The Single Mum's
SURVIVAL GUIDE

The Single Mum's

SURVIVAL GUIDE | How to Pick Up the Pieces and Build a Happy New Life

VIVIENNE SMITH

NEW YORK

The Single Mum's SURVIVAL GUIDE
How to Pick Up the Pieces and Build a Happy New Life

© 2014 VIVIENNE SMITH.

Published in New York, New York, by Morgan James Publishing. Morgan James and The Entrepreneurial Publisher are trademarks of Morgan James, LLC. www.MorganJamesPublishing.com

The Morgan James Speakers Group can bring authors to your live event. For more information or to book an event visit The Morgan James Speakers Group at www.TheMorganJamesSpeakersGroup.com.

A FREE eBook edition is available
with the purchase of this print book

CLEARLY PRINT YOUR NAME IN THE BOX ABOVE

Instructions to claim your free eBook edition:
1. Download the BitLit app for Android or iOS
2. Write your name in UPPER CASE in the box
3. Use the BitLit app to submit a photo
4. Download your eBook to any device

ISBN 978-1-61448-826-2 paperback
ISBN 978-1-61448-827-9 eBook
ISBN 978-1-61448-828-6 hardcover
Library of Congress Control Number:
2013957031

Cover Design by:
Chris Treccani
www.3dogdesign.net

Interior Design by:
Bonnie Bushman
bonnie@caboodlegraphics.com

In an effort to support local communities, raise awareness and funds, Morgan James Publishing donates a percentage of all book sales for the life of each book to Habitat for Humanity Peninsula and Greater Williamsburg.

Get involved today, visit
www.MorganJamesBuilds.com

Habitat
for Humanity®
Peninsula and
Greater Williamsburg
Building Partner

For single mums everywhere — including the ones whose stories feature on these pages. Please remember: you are not alone!

CONTENTS

PREFACE

I was once where you are now – first after a 15 year relationship, with a three year old and a three week old baby, when my husband suddenly announced that he'd been having an affair and was leaving and then later (this time of course with older children) when I plucked up the courage to leave my disastrous second marriage to a sometimes charming but abusive man who had a string of bad debts and was taking full advantage of my (and my family's) generosity. I've had times where every day was a struggle but I knew deep down that it would be OK in the end – and it was. Just at the time I'd finally resigned myself to being single forever I met my lovely husband (it's third time lucky for me!). I always felt very strongly that there must be something good to come out of so much pain and heartache, that I must be able to put all my experience to good use in helping and supporting other single mums. I also talked extensively to other single mums. Some of their stories are featured here on these pages. This book is the result of everything we have learned and experienced.

After the break-up of my second marriage I received this wonderful letter from my counsellor. I hope that these words will inspire you, because so much of what she says will apply to *you*, too.

"What a distressing time you've been having, and what an understatement I've just made. I'm so relieved to hear that you are now free of X, back in your own home with locks changed and hopefully slowly managing to get back to normality. You have

a lot going for you-energy, talent, good looks, a supportive and loving family and two wonderful sons. Your time with X was not a mistake, but a learning curve-despite all the dreadful things that happened, notice the strengths it brought out in you, and it did bring out strengths, you've kept your home, your sons are safe and so are you, all these things take strength of character and persistence, and such strengths applied in different ways will give you a wonderful future if you grant yourself that gift!!I imagine you are now having to consider divorce or are perhaps in the midst of arranging one-I think that once you are legally free, you'll feel even better. Of course it's sad that your relationship with X ended as it did and you will feel sad about this-don't be ashamed to grieve, it's a normal process even after the most horrendous relationship-we grieve what we thought the relationship was going to be and the fact that it didn't turn out that way and that's what makes it 'normal. It goes without saying that I wish you every success for the future–you deserve it."

ACKNOWLEDGEMENTS

I wish to thank the following contributing experts, who so generously allowed me to use extracts from their work or in some cases, wrote a special piece for inclusion in this book:

Sue Atkins
Wilma Allan
Gemma Hope
Francine Kaye
Suzy Miller
Marina Pearson
Jonathan Roche
Rosalind Sedacca
Dawn Tarter

I also want to express my deep gratitude to all the courageous single parents who shared their stories with me – this book is all the richer for your wisdom, honesty, humour and hard-won experience. I salute you.

CHAPTER ONE

DEALING WITH THE BREAK-UP

Whether It's Your Decision Or His

"Why love if losing hurts so much? I have no answers anymore; only the life I have lived. The pain now is part of the happiness then."

—Anthony Hopkins

"In order to have great happiness you have to have great pain and unhappiness - otherwise how would you know when you're happy?"

—Leslie Caron

Kayleigh *I was actually engaged to my son's dad and broke off the engagement. It was probably about a month after I broke it off with him that I found out that I was going to have my baby and at that point the reasons that I had for breaking up were so strong that I didn't feel that I could really move forward and change my mind about that just because I was having a child. I felt like I'd made the right decision; I still do, because I think it would have ended up in divorce and I wouldn't have been happy so I did it from the very beginning. We were never married and I was a single mother from day one and that was tough. When I was 23 I remember I was very brave, I wasn't afraid to be a mom because of course I had no idea what I was getting into – I was pregnant, I was going to have a baby and I was very happy about it. Had I known exactly what it entailed I think I would have been scared to death but I had no clue! I lived with my parents the first couple of years before I moved out here. I think one challenge was that I was still young and I think that being around my friends, who had yet to get married and who still had their free time and still had their freedom was a little difficult. It's not that I needed to go out all the time but I felt a little bit cut off. I lost touch with some of them and I felt like I was a bit of an outsider, compared to before. Sometimes we didn't have the same focus or things to talk about and everybody was so young and here I was, I had this baby to take care of. So that was a little challenging just feeling like an outsider for a while. They weren't doing anything to make me feel that way, that's just how I felt and it took a bit of time to realise: this is my life and look at what I have, instead of what I've had to give up. And what was I really giving up anyway?*

I can't emphasize enough what a help my parents were, opening up their house to me and helping me with my son. Living with the sounds of a crying baby at night all over again, babysitting, the toys and playpen and highchair and all the other things needed invading their space, and being supportive of me. My best friend at the time was also trying to get pregnant but hadn't had any luck yet. She was always there for my son and me. It was so nice to have her to shop with or to visit or to just talk. I usually brought my son with me and she loved being an "Aunt". She was the one who made me feel connected again. She just always made me feel so comfortable. She had her son a few years later.

Emer *I had my daughter when I was 21 and in the second year of college. They allowed me to finish up early at Easter because she was born in April. At that stage I was still with her dad. We'd only been going out about ten months before we* went travelling and I became pregnant. I had her in April and then I went back to Uni in September and completed my third year, my degree year. That was quite a tough year going back and her dad was looking after her at home. We broke up then when she was about one. It just wasn't working and he was more of a child than she was! I found it extremely frustrating. So we broke up but we've both maintained, as much as we can, a good working relationship. I worked really hard to keep that communication open and make sure that he was around as much as he could be.

She was born with Downs Syndrome. When she was born the nurses alerted the doctors and we were pretty much told as soon as she was born that they had their suspicions. I was waiting for about a week to get the blood test confirmation from the hospital but I think we knew anyway. I think it was day six that we were told for definite. They were very supportive but she had two holes in her heart, so obviously all the medical symptoms that go with Downs Syndrome were a massive worry. However, she did really, really well; I think they said that my breast-feeding helped (it's quite unusual for babies with Downs to be able to breastfeed). At the beginning it's that not knowing, never having had any contact with the Syndrome or the symptoms, so I was kind of starting from scratch. I had books and people came…there's an organisation in Galway called the Brothers of Charity and they were fantastic. There's just a lot of extra stuff. There are a lot of extra medical check-ups, there were a lot of extra developmental classes in terms of her physical development and also sign language, to help her communicate sooner. She was actually an excellent baby, but you knew that you had to work a little bit harder. There are lots of extra problems that go with Downs. Her immune system was not strong; her thyroid levels have always been a concern. There was talk of keyhole surgery at one stage but the holes in her heart did, luckily, sort themselves out. She's eleven next week and she's doing well but the gap in school is getting bigger and bigger. She's coming home with homework that she's not able to do and I have to adapt it, so I think we'll keep her in mainstream schooling for as long as we can but we have noticed the gap getting bigger. She does have great support at the school. She's got a one-to-one helper who's with her all the time. She's starting High School in September and she's going to a school that have had quite a few Downs children go through the system, so they've got a good unit set up, which should support keeping her in mainstream.

Jennifer I remember him showing me a photograph once, and saying "this is X" and I just thought she was one of the friends he volunteered on the charity with.

I must have thought it was odd at the time because I still remember the expression on his face. It was almost like he wanted my approval! But I dismissed it instantly because I trusted him and we were happily married (or so I thought). I remember the evening my husband told me like it was yesterday. My little boy was sound asleep after his busy day. We'd just finished dinner and were sitting side by side on the sofa whilst I breast fed our baby girl. It happened quite out of the blue. "We need to talk", he said. Apparently he'd met someone else over two years ago, they'd been having an affair and now he was leaving me. I couldn't take it in at all. Apparently he felt we'd been "jogging along" for the last couple of years and although we still got on, he felt the spark had gone. Incidentally, perhaps I could ring my parents and get them to come and collect me, as we obviously couldn't both sleep under the same roof that night. I obediently phoned my parents and then stumbled upstairs like a sleepwalker to pack some things for myself and the baby. Trying to shake my sense of unreality and disbelief, I forced myself to acknowledge the truth and mark this moment by looking in the mirror. I could barely recognise the ashen-faced stranger looking back at me. My parents arrived and as you can imagine, there was a heated exchange between them and my husband. "You bloody fool", my father spluttered, "of course the spark has gone. You've got a tiny baby and a young son.

Things change. Grow up! I'd bet you a million pounds that you'll look at this other woman after 2 children and many years together and not feel like Love's Young Dream! This is real life. You have a family together. Jennifer loves you. She's always been a good and loyal wife. For God's sake don't throw it all away for some foolish infatuation". My husband refused to look any of us in the eye and just kept muttering things like: "I couldn't help it. It just happened. It's bigger than the both of us. There's nothing I can do about it." Realising that I was struggling and in shock, my Mum took the baby in her arms. I couldn't bear to let my husband anywhere near her and screamed "don't touch her!" when he tried. We were clearly going to get nothing resolved that night. My parents left with me and the baby, having got my husband to agree to take our son and stay with his parents for a few days (to see if they could talk some sense into him). It was clear to everyone, including me, that I would struggle to cope with looking after one child just at that moment, let alone two.

Annabel *In a nutshell, I guess I'd suspected something for a while but my husband was a very good actor, so if I mentioned something he'd laugh it off and say: "Don't be so ridiculous" and then we got to one weekend where he was behaving* *slightly oddly. They worked together, so it was so easy. He was her boss, she worked for him. He was in the shower once and he got a text message from her and I read it. It said something jokey and intimate. I was really frantic, so when he got out the shower I confronted him and said "What the hell is that?" And he went: "I've got absolutely no idea. She's obviously just sent it to the wrong person" and he phoned her then and there, in front of me and said "I have this really weird text message from you. I think you must have sent it to the wrong person" and I could hear her speaking and then he said "No, don't worry. Quite funny, really! See you Monday." He was so plausible. He had the opportunity then to tell me everything. But he chose not to. My children really like her. That's another reason why they'd find it hard to believe anything bad about her. I was away with work for three days and he was at home with the children. It sounds ridiculous, but it was all around the fact that our pony was having a foal and this work colleague had already had two foals with her horse, so she said she'd be on hand to help. Anyway, in the end the foal was born before I went away, so that was all fine but I got a phone call from my husband to say: "I just thought I'd let you know that I forgot to cancel her, so she's still coming over". At which point I just thought that was really weird – why would you have a work colleague coming over when you didn't actually need their help? As the day went on, I started to put 2 and 2 together and make 84 in my mind and I decided I'd have to go home early. So I said to the woman I was working for "I'm afraid there's something really important that I really have to do" and I jumped in the car and drove back home. I got there at 9 o'clock at night and obviously I wasn't expected, but her car was still outside and all the curtains and blinds in the house were closed, so I knew there was something going on because we lived in the middle of nowhere and we never closed every single one in the house—only in the room we were in. So I went round the back of the house, peeked through the curtains and I could see them sitting there on the sofa, arm in arm. I let myself into the house and waited until they'd gone to bed and obviously, they went into our bedroom—which felt really strange, and then I steeled myself and walked in and found them in bed together, which precipitated the whole course of events. Our children were asleep down the corridor (I had checked on them to make sure they were asleep and they didn't know what was going on). So she got up and left and I said to him "You'll have to face the music in the morning". Actually, even though that huge betrayal had happened, to begin with, a few weeks down the line, I was willing to try and make a go of it. You don't even see properly what they've done somehow, you just want it all to be as it was. It's total instinct and I was really frightened. I* remember feeling like a shallow person for feeling frightened and thinking straight away: what am I going to do and how will I be financially, how will I be able to cope with everything? It sounds really mercenary but actually those are the things that you really worry about. You're really worried about the security of your family but I didn't say to myself: Do I really love this person, do I want to stay with this person now? It wasn't about that, it was about keeping the family together, regardless of what had happened. The decision in the end was made for me. He said he's stop seeing her; he'd moved out into this rented place down the road, which was really weird. Of course, I didn't really believe him and he also told me on the night that I found them that he's had lots of affairs, all during our marriage, so then I realised that he was a serial adulterer. I started making sure I drove past this rented house he was in (which was on the school run) to see when he was there; I became obsessive about it, which was weird because I'm not normally like that but the thing is: I **had** to know. I had four great girlfriends who were brilliant and all rallied round. I had suspected that he wasn't being truthful about where he was. But he told me that he was at home and at 6 o'clock in the morning one of the girls had driven past his house and his car wasn't there; it was obvious he'd just strung me along with a whole heap of rubbish but he wanted me to make the decision and I did. Because it's all about guts and facing up to something that's unpalatable. I remember just ringing him and saying: "Look, you're still lying." I just said: "That's it. It's all over." We know a couple where she had the affair and they patched it up but eventually split up three months ago and their sons are 18 and 17. Everyone is blaming him for it now because he's gone off with a much younger girl but he confided in my husband and said that the problem was that he'd just never got over her affair. He still thinks about it every day. He said that he should have ended the relationship when he found out about her affair, should have known that it was always going to be a problem. I know some people do, but once the trust is broken I don't know how people go back.

Jennifer I know now that he cheated on me before we got married and maybe he had more than one affair when we were married. Looking back, there was definitely a work colleague that he was very close to. I once found out by chance that he'd left work early to spend the afternoon with her because she was leaving the company. At the time he assured me that he loved me far too much to ever jeopardise our relationship. But these days, knowing what I know about him now, I wouldn't be too sure. I don't think my ex has been tempted to cheat again since he remarried. His *current wife (or his Mum) would kill him! And surely even he is not stupid enough to start a third family?!*

Angela *I had a friend whose husband left her when she was pregnant with their second child and she had an18-month-old. How can you even think that it's alright to leave someone at that point?*

Annabel *Now I wonder what I ever saw in him. I must have not known what I was doing in my 20s but that's the thing that I think has come out of this: you know yourself so much better in your 30s and 40s and you're much better able to choose the right person. It's so nice to be a young parent but on the other hand so many relationships go wrong when you get together too young. He wasn't happy because I made him feel inadequate. I was always so ambitious and he just wanted to have a good time. He's been through so many jobs. He spent a whole two years after we split up, pretending he was going to do something really incredible but it never came to anything…It's really funny now, because my business is going well and there must be part of him that thinks: I should probably have stayed, so that's quite funny! My mother said: "We would never have said anything at the time but he was just hanging on to your coat tails." I do have moments where I feel sorry for him. What's been quite good for me is to understand that. And I did go and see a counsellor at the time about everything and she was brilliant. She said "Look: the fact of the matter is that it takes two people for a relationship to break down. You allowed him to get away with bloody murder. He didn't talk to you about anything but you didn't talk to him about anything either. And you let him behave in the way that he did. He never did anything around the house; he never helped with the children. What on earth were you doing, allowing that to happen?" And I suppose it was a bit like that. Also, my parents don't have a passionate marriage so I wasn't used to seeing that. What I had in my first marriage was probably very similar to what my parents had. So for me, I wasn't unhappy. I might not have been passionately in love with him but actually a big part of me thought: well, maybe that's what happens. And he needed a more passionate, more physical relationship. I don't even think he has that grand passion any more in his current situation because I don't think that intense passion does last but that's presumably why he had so many affairs- he was seeking to recreate that passion all the time because you can't sustain that. Right now he works in London Monday to Friday and she's back in their place in the country. I wonder if that's why* *they're finally getting married, because she's feeling insecure or getting itchy feet. I don't know .It's really interesting to surmise...*

Angela *I couldn't work, which was hard because I'm dedicated to my kids at school but I just had another meltdown, I couldn't work for a while. The counsellor said it: "You're fired, you don't have a role" and that was harsh. I came back from the counselling session in tears and my older kids said "You don't need to go there any more" but what she said was true, so I would advise anyone to go to somebody who is going to tell them things they may not want to hear but that are true, rather than just saying "Oh yes, you can fix this". You can't fix everything. Find something that you can do, like journaling, where you can talk your way through situations. It's a long time but you can come out the other end eventually.*

Andrea *My husband used to talk a lot about this poor woman at work who had a really awful husband, how he let her take care of everything round the house and didn't lift a finger to help. He was forever going on about her and I remember saying to him, quite innocently "Don't you think you're getting a bit too involved in her life?" If only I'd known how right I was! I first found out there was something wrong when my father died. I was in bed, crying, and I couldn't understand why my husband wouldn't comfort me. He just turned round and said "I don't think I love you any more". It was like a dagger in my heart. Of course I asked him lots of questions and he finally admitted that it was her. I was just a mess. He talked to friends and we even went to Relate a few times but he dismissed counselling, saying: "This is rubbish—it's not helping!" In the end he said we should try again so he rang her up and broke it off. I don't remember much about the year that followed. I guess we just plodded on and I tried to pretend everything was normal. But it wasn't really. I still remember getting all dressed up for a party-stockings, suspenders, the whole lot but I just felt really awful. I remember that day the following April. I worked in a clothes shop then and we were launching a big promotion in the store that day. I remember him saying "Good luck with that", just like any normal day. I picked up the children from school on the way home from work and I went to check the answer machine in the kitchen for messages like I always did. There were two envelopes propped up by the phone, one addressed to me and one addressed to the children. I opened mine first. It was all very matter of fact, saying they'd set up home together. He even put their address and contact numbers in. I screamed, I think, and then the children came running in. I* *remember my daughter was completely hysterical. She was just rolling over and over on the floor screaming "No! No!" My sisters came and looked after me and the doctor put me on some "happy pills". I was like a zombie, couldn't eat, couldn't sleep. We had this really horrible meeting in a hotel just after he left. As soon as I laid eyes on him I couldn't stop crying. I was this blubbering mess! I hated him for what he'd done to the children because my Mum left home when I was 15. My daughter was about 17 then, I think, and actually she recovered faster than my son because he was only 14 and he suffered more with no male role model around. I'm not sure if I'll ever get over it. His new wife's always there at big family occasions and it ruins the evening for me. I remember my daughter brought my grandson over to see me recently and he was wearing a new knitted jumper. "That's nice," I commented, "Did you make that?" When I found out that my husband's new wife had actually knitted the jumper, it was all I could do not to rip it off him immediately! The children didn't want to meet her to begin with but after a while they came to terms with it, but I didn't. I ended up on my own for the next six years—I just had no interest in being with anyone else. He was my best friend, he was everything to me and if I'm honest it still hurts."*

Jennifer, Kayleigh and Andrea were all lucky to have the support and care of family in their hour of need. If at all possible, I would recommend that you enlist the help of a loving family member or even best friend. It's not a good time to be alone in the early days and the presence of someone who cares about you can be immensely reassuring, both for you and the children. If there's no one round the corner that can come and keep you company for at least some of the time, make sure you keep in regular telephone touch with your loved ones-an evening telephone call to check in with someone who cares can feel like a lifeline at the moment. It is also a good idea to inform your healthcare provider. I know in my case that my doctor was extremely sympathetic and immediately put me under the care of a counsellor, to help me come to terms with my loss and cope with the bleak aftermath of my husband's departure. Your doctor may also prescribe sleeping pills or anti-depressants (happy pills, as Andrea calls them) and of course your doctor is the most qualified person to judge your individual situation but my advice is to proceed with extreme caution here, so that you are not faced with a tricky withdrawal process further down the line. It is certainly worth investigating some of the natural remedies as well, which do not have harmful side effects or addictive qualities.

Angela My two older children had left school and they were pretty independent. His Mum died and when he went ahead of us he really didn't get us anywhere to live. He fell into the role of being his father's son and it was an emotional abandonment for us—he wasn't there for us, he was in shock; his Mum was only 58. He wouldn't admit that he needed to grieve and he just went running. He was just not his normal self. A massive power struggle then started between us and that's when I started getting in to Louise Hay and self-affirmations because I was a wreck—I was just under the covers howling, it was really surreal! It was the first loss of my husband. He often sabotaged himself. He came from a working class British background and from what I can gather this self-sabotaging can be common behaviour. He trained with his father when his mum died—as a blacksmith, doing all the beautiful wrought iron work and at that time there was a huge trend in wrought iron. In England the house prices crashed and we lost our house there. Seventeen years of paying a mortgage on that house, all gone. So we came back to Canada with four kids and five suitcases and started over. I started teaching and supported him, became the sole breadwinner whilst he pursued this career of metalwork. Then he would give work away, so there were some issues around that, and what was ironic was that because of his metalwork he became Artist in Residence, so we had a free house, a beautiful home and he did workshops for the community and I insisted that we save money to buy a house. So we bought a beautiful house, way beyond his expectations and 6 months later I'm saying to my friend: My husband's just done this huge show in Vancouver, the House and Gardens exhibition, and he hasn't shot himself in the foot! But he did that with the woman that he left me for, which I didn't realise at the time. All we ever talked about every weekend was how to make my husband happy, you know? And he never indicated anything to me that he was dissatisfied. He'd say "Let's go for a walk with the dog" and right up to the end, the day that he left I was coordinating a children's concert and we went to my school and picked up chairs in his truck and he helped me set them up in front of the stage for my show. We took the chairs back to my school, we went to the pub. I bought dinner of course and then we went to my friend's party and then he did it! I said to him: "This is so great, everything's working out so well—it's the best it's been for years" and he just said "Well actually, I need some space." So we backed out of the driveway and came home. Then after that I do remember going down to try and talk to him and he said "I want you out of my life" and he looked stunned and I'm standing there thinking "I just want you *out of my life?! I mean, where is that coming from?"* He left the next day, so it was a total shock. But that's how it happened.

I think the feelings that someone experiences when they are initiating a break up are that they can't face you properly because you know them too well. I also remember thinking at one stage: I'm eloquent, I can explain it to him, I can argue the case for him staying and raising our boys together. I remember thinking: If I just say the right words I can get him to realise, I can get him to come to his senses. But he didn't want to hear, he didn't want to be persuaded, and I remember one day just before he left him saying "Yes, I know we've had a great day. I know we get on well and yes I do find you really attractive and yes, we do have a laugh together but ...." It was as if he was saying: "stop trying to remind me because I don't want to hear, I want that gone, I want to move on. That's what I've decided". What can you do? And the answer is: **nothing**, because you can't control somebody's feelings or actions.

Angela *What was really hard for me was that he didn't tell me he was going with another woman. He wouldn't tell me why he was leaving. Even that day I'd said to him: "Please tell me the truth" and he'd replied "What do you mean"? So it drove me crazy because it didn't make any sense. I had my suspicions but he wouldn't admit it until three months later I just found him at her house. I did a whole detective thing online and I found his truck parked outside her place. It was really awkward. It was about 1.30 in the morning and her mum was visiting from the States and answered the door. My husband and his mistress were staying over this barn where she kept all these llamas. It was so strange I wrote a story about it (I'm doing my Masters in Arts and Education). I went down this driveway and I could hear the phone ringing in her studio above the llamas (she had a craft workshop there, where she used to do craft and felting) and I could hear this scurrying around upstairs as I was walking. I climbed over the fence and I was walking past all these llamas, who were hissing at me as I passed, and I heard his voice. He called my name and I turned the corner, and he was just standing in the moonlight. I just looked at him and I walked away. All I wanted him to know was just: "I know what you're doing. Why wouldn't you just tell me the truth?" and I walked back to my car. I didn't even want to phone my kids and say: "You'll never guess what your Dad's doing!" I just thought: "This is his story to tell".*

So we set up a meeting at my house and he came. I was making tea in the kitchen and he told the kids when he'd fallen in love. My daughter said "I thought something was going on, Dad" but my son just said "What about Mum?" He was just worried about me.

We had a little bit of time, just a bit of time before my first husband finally left and in that time I tried my best to remind him of all the good things we had, all the good things he'd be giving up (which was tough, as I didn't really feel all that great in the circumstances) and I recall thinking that it was like looking at somebody through a very thick pane of glass. I could see him, it was like the children and I were all calling him, but we couldn't reach him. It was so strange. And I don't think he ever really explained to my satisfaction, and however much I analysed it I came to the conclusion that there aren't always pat answers. Maybe he doesn't know. Maybe none of us will ever really know what happened or what went wrong. I do know that he never gave me a chance to put it right, because I would have at least tried.

Annabel I stopped eating and lost loads of weight-I lost about two and a half stone in seven weeks. My body never really recovered from that. I went into early menopause as a result and lost loads of hair, so I had a lot of physical manifestations of the problem. That's still going on now. Because of going into early menopause I'm now on HRT and my hair never grew back. It's awful now. So all those things are things you have to live with, daily reminders of what happened. But he doesn't have to live with any of that. I think he's pleased he was out of it, so perhaps what happened to me is a reminder in a good way for him. But for me: this is my legacy.

I count myself very lucky not to have gone through the traumatic changes that Annabel did, although I also experienced physical manifestations of my mental anguish. The term "broken-hearted" is an accurate one. At first, I found seeing him almost unbearable. He had been a part of me for so many years and now I had to get used to the fact that I could no longer touch him or kiss him because he now "belonged" to someone else. Whilst my brain tried to come to terms with the new situation, my body couldn't seem to register the truth. My arms used to ache to hold him but now I had to keep them clamped to my sides. I remembered hearing stories of people who've had a limb amputated–they still have sensations in their missing limb, even though it's not there any longer.

The week of my husband's departure I had a frightening experience when I suddenly realised that I was going to have to lie down or collapse. I was reassured to read later that this is in fact a common symptom of shock and quite normal. For many weeks I had terrible dreams and woke up each morning feeling nauseous. Interestingly, in my dreams he was present but there was always something wrong. One day I dreamt that I was in a raft on a river and he was standing on the bank. I watched him recede into the distance as the raft moved away from the shore. In another, I was given the choice of starting again with him and I rejected it instinctively and categorically. These dreams gave me hope. I saw them as my subconscious learning to let go of loving him.

Angela So I've always been a big dreamer and everybody I knew thought that he would keep my feet on the ground. I had produced children's albums, I was performing for kids, I had been in a band and my eldest daughter and I had put out an album. I had booked a tour in England in July the March he left, and I just said: he's not going to sabotage the tour. So we went on the first of July and she and I played a festival in Stonehaven and a festival in Yorkshire and we did all our folk clubs and I drove around England in a standard shift, back on the other side of the road. So I think he had changed a lot from who he was in a little village in Norfolk, and he had transformed enormously but he'd just gone as far as he could go and I just scared the hell out of him! He felt threatened by my growth. When one part of the recipe is changed, it doesn't work out – or when one piece of the jigsaw is changed it just doesn't fit. Many years before he left I had come to the realisation that I am who I am and I cannot change who I am. I can't stop dreaming, I can't stop having five different projects on the go at the same time. This is who I am, I couldn't change. So why would I expect that he could change? We always think that the other person should just see our way but we have to see it their way too and allow them to be. So I really like the saying "I am free to be me and you are free to be you". I think everything happens in divine right order and it was just perfect the way it all worked out.

Although I was so desperate for a "Happy Ever After" for me and my sons, even on the honeymoon I realised that my second marriage was a terrible mistake. We were driving in Spain and I'd fallen asleep and I woke up to discover my husband in this terrible rage, all because he'd got lost and the local map we'd bought wasn't very accurate. I'd never seen someone get so angry about something so insignificant, with no provocation. It was a beautiful day and we were in the middle of this stunning landscape of field upon field of sunflowers. We had no agenda to stick to and with anyone else I could have had a good chuckle about the rubbish map and been philosophical about reaching our holiday apartment an hour later than originally planned. A quick dip in the pool and a glass of something cold would have done the trick. But here he was, swearing and punching the car, kicking the tyres, marching up and down, literally ranting and raving. What I saw really chilled me to the bone because I'd seen temper flashes before (but he'd always had an excuse ready for losing his cool) and now deep down I suspected that this was a taste of things to come. I was right. Things got a whole lot worse and I began to get worried, not just for myself but for the children. I also didn't want my boys growing up and thinking it was OK to be abusive and disrespectful to your partner (or anyone, for that matter!). I did initiate counselling but he decided that he didn't need it and it reached the point where I had no choice but to escape from the relationship. So, as a result of my experiences I'd have to say that my own personal philosophy is now that if you have problems in a relationship you owe it to your partner and yourself (not to mention any children you may have had together) to speak up and do your utmost to work the problems out. If you reach a point where you have tried everything you possibly can and it becomes clear that resolving your problems is no longer possible then I believe there is no shame in ending that relationship and seeking happiness elsewhere. So it's true: people *do* change and so do their values and goals and sometimes the two halves of a couple do not change and grow at the same rate. It is up to all of us to look at ourselves in the mirror and say "I did my best and I did everything I could". If you can do that, then you can hold your head up high and know that you acted with integrity, whether you chose to leave or whether you were left.

Elaine To be honest with you, he always used to drink a lot but then we all did in our early 20s. So I never thought much of it, but shortly after my first child was born it started to get worse. Maybe it was the pressure of having children or the fact that his father was an alcoholic, I don't know (because his father was an alcoholic too) but anyway, that's when it all started to kick off. By the time my second child was born he'd lost his job and had been caught drinking and driving. It was when my second child was five that we did finally split, and it was very much my decision. He didn't want to split up at all. When he was drunk, the next day he'd have no recognition of what he'd done or how bad he'd been, so it was "What did I do wrong?" and that I can kind of understand. I don't know if there was a straw that broke the camel's back. It went on and on… One of the reasons that I have stayed on my own and been happy staying on my own is that: to get away from that situation was such an utter relief that I wouldn't want to put myself through it again. It was an absolute relief and almost a joy for me to get away from that situation, however hard it was to take that decision and sort things out. The one bit of advice I'd give my old self is: I should have done it sooner (i.e. left my husband) In my situation, the right course of action was staring me in the face. I'd say don't be afraid to do what you think is right. If you've got children I'd also say that the most important thing is to give them a happy background and upbringing.

Maggie *I'd had warning bells right from the start of our relationship. He was charming and clever but a bit of a rebel, too. They say women fall for a bad boy and I must say I loved that edge. But then things started to happen which troubled me. He always had a ready explanation or excuse for why he'd lost his temper or said something horrible, or made a rude comment about one of the children…he was tired, he'd driven all those miles to come and see me, he wasn't feeling well, he didn't mean it really, I was imagining it–he hadn't really done or said that. I guess I was just too trusting and gullible and I did so want that "happy ever after". The thing that most bothered me was that he didn't get on with my son. I had to admit that my little boy was playing up–but then what child wouldn't, with a dominant man arriving in the household and trying to lay down the law all the time? I found myself constantly playing piggy in the middle and feeling helplessly torn. On at least two occasions I decided that enough was enough and tried to end the relationship because I could see that my son was unhappy. But each time he'd do a massive charm offensive and promise to do whatever it took to make things work. Both times he shamelessly wheedled, manipulated, browbeat me, guilt-tripped me and eventually wore me down. He even enlisted the rest of my family to persuade me that I should give him a chance. After all, he could be so lovely when he wanted to be. There seemed to be so much potential and he'd had a tough upbringing. It wasn't his fault. He could change. And once we were married it would all be rosy. I'm an optimist, you see! But after* the wedding his temper got worse and his mood changes became more extreme. He began to humiliate me in front of strangers and then friends (although never in front of my parents or sisters, who continued to have a soft spot for him). Slowly but surely, the process of my isolation had begun. Then I found out gradually about all the bad things lurking in his past. These ranged from two ex-wives and an extra sister that he never admitted to, to failed businesses and bad debts. Now it became clear why he was so keen to relocate from one end of the country to another—he was running away, reinventing himself as he went along. I started to become really scared of him. I never left the kids alone with him and tried to stand up to his frequent bouts of temper and ill humour. He never hit me but he swore and said vicious, belittling things. I sometimes felt that it would be better if he actually hit me, because then there would be something to show for it—some form of proof-instead of his words going round and round in my head and the knowledge that someone who professed to love me could act as if he hated me more than anything on earth. He would be cold, critical and angry with me and harass and harangue me until I cried, and then come and comfort me. I was so confused and lacking in confidence by this time that I even allowed him to do this. I no longer knew which way was up. The next day I'd be emotionally drained but he'd act as if nothing had happened. Every day was torture as I had a continuous loop of questions in my head—"Should I try harder? Is it my fault? Should I give him a chance?

Should I end it?" I distinctly remember a day when I felt such dread at going home to him that I considered just driving off the side of a bridge and ending it all. He finally agreed to see a counsellor with me, but walked out after a few sessions, declaring it all a "waste of time". But the counsellor was on to him - she had his measure and she warned me that he had a personality disorder and it was going to get worse as he found it increasingly hard to suppress or hide his "dark side". I was so lucky to find out about a women's advice service that helped victims of domestic abuse. They told me he was a textbook example of an abuser and warned me of the risk of staying too long. The most frightening thing was to hear that the majority of murders in cases where a male partner is abusive come when the woman has stated her desire to be free. It seems that the abuser senses that he is losing control and this can send him over the edge into violence. I began to make my escape plan. When I finally plucked up the courage to ask him to leave, he refused to go. So began a terrifying stalemate which lasted for four surreal months. When he left the house he never told me where he was going and he'd arrive back with no warning. Sometimes he would treat me *with icy hatred and at others, do his utmost to woo me back into his bed. I tried to keep things as normal as possible for the children but the strain was unbearable. Things finally came to a head one evening. The kids were (thank goodness) away for the weekend. I was getting ready for an evening out with a friend. When he returned to the house it was clear that he had been drinking heavily. He was verbally aggressive and calling me all sorts of vile words. When I refused to stay and listen, he followed me into my bedroom and proceeded to smash everything up. He swept all my bottles off the dressing table and started pulling out the contents of all my drawers. There was a lamp with a heavy ceramic base by my bedside. He picked it up and smashed it against the wall, advancing on me in a menacing way. I was completely rooted to the spot and it wasn't until he took me by the throat and flipped me backwards on to the bed that my instincts kicked in and I tried to kick him off. He could have raped me or killed me at that moment because I was unable to escape his grip around my neck. He kept me in this stranglehold long enough to make this point before shoving me off the bed and onto the floor. Then he went downstairs to watch TV! I sat there shaking for a while before summoning up the presence of mind to pack some things and go outside to wait for my friend. I called the police from the safety of her car. We watched as they took him away in handcuffs. The nice policeman told me later that he claimed he had been "acting in self-defence"! But for me that incident had a silver lining because it finally got him out of my life for good.*

"There was a time in the marriage when I could no longer look at myself in a mirror, couldn't feel I was a nice person. A bad relationship can do that, can make you doubt everything good you ever felt about yourself."

—Dionne Warwick

"Some cause happiness wherever they go; others whenever they go."

—Oscar Wilde

Alanis is singing it all for me—"I recommend getting your heart trampled on to anyone" (in my case it felt more like a machete job); "Waiting for deliverance" (the "Oh God somebody please come and rescue me" stage); "I don't want to be a Band-

Aid if the wound is not mine" (Jesus – how can he save me – he's got more emotional baggage than I have!); "The cross I bear that you gave to me" (No-one can do that victim-thing better than a woman scorned). Anger and pain that seemed to shred me from the inside out. A slow, crippling, crumbling of the core of my body that I didn't even know existed within me. For me, this was my first taste of bereavement.

Obviously, after all that had happened, my shattered sense of self-worth was screaming for a shag–but fortunately, the offers on hand were by people who seemed even more lost and confused than I was. I managed to steer clear–more by luck than judgement–through that first clichéd hurdle. I went through the "Oh, he's bound to realise what he's done and try to make another go of it" phase. But he didn't. Meanwhile, I was experiencing the early stages of panic attacks, and a weird sensation that time was moving far more slowly than it ever had before.

It finally dawned on me–I was in grief. I had never had any one truly close to me die before, but this was the closest thing. I had lost a whole life–past and future. Gone in an incomprehensible instant. Always thinking it might reappear around the next corner – but gradually realising that that part of me was gone forever. So I did what my many wise friends were encouraging me to do–I got real.

I had the blessing of so many fantastic friends–friends I didn't even know I had–who gave so much more than just emotional support and the time to listen. They were brave enough to be honest with me–comments like "God, what's happened to you is so awful I can't help laughing" were strangely helpful. I also loved the response from one dear friend, after the guilt I had been feeling of dumping such awful news on my family and friends. When I told her that I was now joining the club of single motherhood, she said with great passion and absolutely no tact–"FANTASTIC!" But my friends also prevented my tackling of the mundane realities–possible financial holocaust; children torn out of school–from leaving me devoid of hope, and they helped me to believe that the world still had some good stuff waiting for me up ahead.

I was fighting. I moved out, got a place to rent, started panicking about my future. But I was still the victim fighting against the odds–and the trouble with that is you just never get your act together, because it's always someone else's fault. It's only when you face up to the horrifying reality of a situation that you can truly take it in hand–and own it. You make it your own. It's no-one else's fault or responsibility if you don't make things work out. I looked the worse-case scenarios of every aspect of my life right in the face–and made whatever provisions I could. And somehow, by making that appointment with the Lone Parent Advisor, with my youngest child screaming *throughout most of the interview (no toys provided or changing room), applying for State Benefits, and enrolling the kids in schools I hadn't previously wanted them to go to, took the fear away. It didn't mean "that was it —it just meant I was taking back some control. And you know the amazing thing? Even though it took a real leap of faith, and a good helping of black humour, to really start taking control of my life, the more I did it, the more I believed it was going to work out somehow. And the most amazing thing for me was that other people seemed to be drawn in and they began to believe it too.*

Strange as it may sound, it was the children who helped the most, because they forced me to take back control of the present. I didn't have the luxury of descending into total emotional free-fall. There were these very strong brave little people who needed me to make things work out for them. They kept me sane in other ways too. When your partner has acted as if the past ten years was merely a passing of time without any emotional consequence, you really begin to question whether you have imagined the whole thing. But the children lie as physical evidence of something beautiful that no mid-life crisis can obliterate. A good friend sent me off on an excellent motivational course. Boy was I ready for that. It was like someone had handed me a load of really useful tools to continue turning my life around even more dramatically than I already had done—and getting rid of all those stupid self-limiting beliefs that I didn't know I had. Now that I wasn't a "mother of three in a stable relationship with a house and two cars", I had the opportunity to become anything I wanted. Of course, I could have done all that before, but oh, the children are so exhausting and the house has to be finished *and the list of excuses for not thinking about my own personal growth were endless. People would ask me "How do you cope on your own?" But strangely, having one less adult to care for actually made my life easier. Also, not having to bear the burden of someone else's unhappiness that neither of us had really been able to acknowledge—well that was like a massive weight lifted from my shoulders. I got rid of all my excuses and allowed myself to dream of what I wanted, with ambition instead of frustrated regret. I had become free. I had become myself again.*

I did have one tricky problem for a while. No one tells you what to do with your ex-partner. You're supposed to hate and despise them—they are the reason behind every sorrow in your life. It was all so horribly negative, and somehow, the children took me from the bitterness of the usual break-up mentality and gave me every reason to fight for something better. When you have a living reminder of unconditional love each day, it makes you question the quality of the love that you think has now broken your heart. And that was yet another revelation – it's not 'love' that causes the pain. Love is a good thing. What causes the pain—and so many problems within relationships of all kinds–is being 'needy'. That was not a person I wanted to be any longer. After ten years of learning to live with someone in love, in seemed so crazy just to give it all up because I now wanted to find *a new way to live with them—albeit separately. I* finally *realised that posing 'unanswerable questions' and re-examining the past ad nauseam were clearly not getting me anywhere. I decided to let the love that had kept us together for ten years be the guiding factor with keeping us healthily and positively apart. The children were a constant reminder that anger and self-pity and doubt and fear–in other words, parenthood –can all be balanced with, well, love.*

I was lucky enough to be able to put down a deposit on a house and get out of the Benefit trap – thank God for interest-only mortgages. I make the house 'work' for me by taking in lodgers, though some of my friends are keeping a book out on how long each one will last. I enrolled on a training course that takes up almost every Saturday for the next two years and THEN organised the childcare, knowing that was the only way I would make it happen. I am home schooling one of my kids and loving it. So I'm sitting in the bath and I've finally *managed to blubber a bit, and I'm wondering how to describe that odd feeling I have when I'm all alone in the house and the kids are quiet in their beds. A kind of familiar feeling that seems to be growing stronger all the time–that precious time that I have for myself. I think I can only describe it as–"Freedom".*

Suzy Miller, the "Alternative Divorce Guide" is the creator of **The Starting Over Show,** http://startingovershow.co.uk/

Alternative Divorce Guide, www.alternativedivorceguide.com ,

Divorce in a Box UK http://startingovershow.co.uk/divorce-in-a-box/ and **Divorce in a Box USA** http://divorceinabox.us

"You may have a fresh start any moment you choose, for this thing that we call "failure" is not the falling down, but the staying down."

—Mary Pickford

CHAPTER TWO

TELLING THE KIDS

Here is the story of how world-renowned expert Rosalind Sedacca broke the news to *her* son and in the process created her highly-acclaimed guide for parents. I wish I had discovered her guide in my hour of need and I urge you to consider using it yourself.

Breaking the Divorce News to My Son
Was a Trauma That Transformed My Life!
By Rosalind Sedacca

I've faced many difficult moments in my life. But preparing to tell my son that I will be divorcing his father was absolutely one of the worst.

He was innocent--a sweet eleven year old who loved both his parents dearly. He didn't deserve this.

I struggled with anxiety for weeks. When should we tell him? What should we say?

How do you tell a child that the life he has known is about to be disrupted—forever? How do you tell him that it's not his fault?

And how do you prepare him for all the unknowns looming ahead when you're not sure yourself how it will turn out?

One night I had an idea that resonated powerfully for me. I could prepare a storybook for my son. I could use photos and words to talk about our family—from before he was born to the present preparing him for the new changes ahead.

The storybook would give him something to hold on to, and read over again. It would explain why this was happening and what to expect. Rather than stumbling through the conversation, it would give me a written script well thought through in advance.

When I completed the storybook and showed my husband, he approved. It wasn't judgmental or accusatory. Instead it told the truth while focusing on messages of mutual agreement—the love and concern we had for our son.

While my husband was angry about many issues, he agreed the storybook was a smart idea. We decided to present it together.

There is no way to make this tough conversation an easy one. As I started reading about the changes in our family, tears pooled up in my son's eyes. By the time we reached the end, he was weeping and clinging tightly to both of us.

And then, as a family, we talked, cried, hugged, answered questions, reread important passages and consoled one another.

Having the book to hold on to was helpful for my son. We discussed the impending divorce many times in the next weeks and months, often rereading sections in the book as a reminder that things will be okay.

*It's been more than a decade since I prepared that storybook. It became the basis for my internationally acclaimed book, **How Do I Tell the Kids about the Divorce? A Create-a-Storybook Guide to Preparing Your Children--with Love!** I provide the text, along with age-appropriate fill-in-the-blank templates, so other parents can customize with their own family history while sharing the essential messages they want their children to hear.*

I've since founded the Child-Centered Divorce Network for parents which provides my free e-zine, blog, coaching services, advice and other valuable resources related to divorce and parenting issues.

My now-grown son has gotten married and is a successful veterinarian. He's still quite close to his father and me. He honored me by writing the Foreword to my book and on occasion has been present to address audiences when I've spoken at Divorce Expos, conferences and other events for parents.

Of course, he hasn't a clue about just how much that means to me—but as a divorced parent reading this story, I know you do!

Extract from **"Telling kids about divorce? Avoid these mistakes"** *by Rosalind Sedacca.*

Rosalind Sedacca, Founder of the Child-Centered Divorce Network, is a Divorce & Parenting Coach and author of *How Do I Tell the Kids about the Divorce? A Create-a-Storybook Guide to Preparing Your Children – with Love!*

To learn more about the e-book, visit http://www.howdoitellthekids. com. For her free e-book on Post-Divorce Parenting, free e-zine, coaching services and other valuable resources on divorce and parenting issues, visit: www.childcentereddivorce.com

For me, the most heart-breaking thing of all was finding the strength to tell my three year old (who totally worshipped his Dad) that his father had left. This is such a personal thing and how you tell your children will necessarily be dictated by their age, the circumstances of the split and the willingness of your ex-partner to be involved in breaking the news. In my case it was down to me to explain what was happening. My son was so young and I found the situation incredibly hard, given that I myself was struggling to accept what had happened.

In the end I did it in stages over a few days, starting with "Daddy's at work", then "Daddy's staying in London" to "Daddy lives in London now". At each stage I repeated that his Daddy loved him and his brother very much and mentioned exactly when Daddy would be coming to see them. As time went on I explained that we were getting divorced, using the same reassurances that his Daddy loved them both very much. At the time I found it impossible to tell an untruth or imply that the decision was mutual, nor did I want to talk about his affair, so I said that Daddy no longer wanted to be married to Mummy and then later that he wanted to be married to … instead.

Children of any age will need reassurance and help to adapt to the situation. After all, the child is dealing with a decision its parents have made–one that he or she has no control over and in most cases most definitely does *not* agree with! I remember reading that children often

have terrible anxiety over questions such as: What's Daddy doing now? Where does he sleep and who's looking after him? If you can summon up the strength and patience, try to elicit any burning questions your child may have about these arrangements. It may be of tremendous comfort. As the main carer for your child, you can also expect to bear the brunt of their feelings about this traumatic event in his or her life. Again, it will require a lot of strength and patience and understanding on your part not to take this personally but instead to help him or her to feel the feelings and express them in order to let them go. Sometimes a book or toy will allow a younger child to express feelings in an indirect way, which can be easier for them. One excellent book I found is called:

Dinosaurs Divorce: A Guide for Changing Families (Dino Life Guides for Families) by Laurene Krasny Brown and Marc Brown

There are also excellent books for older children and teenagers available from Amazon or your local bookstore.

One thing that I discovered was that if my child became really upset because he was missing his Dad, this could be alleviated by having a phone call. Just hearing his dad's voice seemed to calm him and of course these days a Skype call is both free and easy to arrange if you both have a computer and webcam. My present husband's two children live with their mother in Germany and finances do not allow for frequent visits, so Skype has been a marvellous way to keep in contact, see their latest art work and chat about how school is going.

Maggie *For me, telling my kids was easy because they'd known for a long time that things weren't good. My eldest daughter was just relieved, I think because she never got on with her stepfather. Even my younger daughter, who had been his favourite, accepted his absence with minimum fuss. There'd been an incident before he left where he completely lost his temper with her over something small and swore at her and shoved her. I think that shocked her as much as me because he'd never done that before. I knew it meant he was getting worse. She was a bit emotional for a couple of weeks after he left but I told her teacher at school and between us we just kept a special eye on her and cut her some slack if she was behaving out of character. I think for all of us that there was this sense of a dark cloud having been lifted once he'd gone and we all felt safer and more relaxed at home, instead of walking on eggshells all the time. I think it helped that they could see how happy I was to have life peaceful and normal again.*

Emer *She was only one when we broke up and in some ways I think that's a blessing in disguise because you do see older children who don't deal with the changes well, it's quite hard for them to take it in, whereas in my daughter's case it's all she's known. We talk about it a lot, especially because of the project I did, and we openly discuss our plans for the week. She gets very excited about going to both our houses, which is great. I think the only big conversation which I'm not looking forward to is the one about her understanding her disability. Her analytical ability isn't very strong anyway, so her questioning level would be fairly basic. The most complex question she's asked is about Granny and Grandad passing on and they're still alive, so she's kind of aware of age but in terms of us: I think she's quite happy. Her dad's got a girlfriend as well and we've got our family here and it works quite well. I can imagine questions cropping up down the line, but as it stands now, we're getting away with it!*

Jennifer *My little boy took the news really badly. He cried when I put him to bed and said there were monsters in his room. He went from being totally dry at night to wetting the bed every night. His behaviour veered from withdrawn to aggressive to clingy. One night I had an argument with his father on the phone. I thought he was asleep but he must have crept out of bed and listened on the stairs. I went upstairs afterwards to check on him and found him huddled miserably under my duvet, comfort-eating all the chocolates from his Advent calendar.*

Annabel *I had to tell the children what had happened and why, but in a way they could understand. So I couldn't say to them "Oh, I found Daddy in bed with someone" because they were 4 and 6. But I did sit my daughter down and say something like: "You know when you have your best friend at school and then someone new joins the class and they decide that they're going to be best friend and your best friend doesn't really want to be friends with you any more, because they've got someone they think is better? It's a bit like that. Daddy was my best friend but then someone else came along and she decided that she wanted Daddy to be her best friend and he didn't know how to be friends with both of us." And she said "That's not very nice" and I said "No-it's not and you must never do that!" But now of course I realise **he's** slowly over time said to her: "Well, Mummy and I weren't very happy together and we're both much happier as we are now, so it's been a really good solution" and I feel like saying "One day I am going to tell her exactly what happened and how it felt!" But my daughter doesn't want it to be like it was, so I don't tell her the truth at the moment because I don't think she wants to hear it. She's not ready to hear it.*

Elaine *The children would start to ask questions about what had happened and probably blaming me for things, asking "Why isn't my dad here?"*

Rachel *He is more aware of the situation now and, although no doubt would like to see his father, he is under no illusions about the situation. I was very protective when he was small and would not say very much about the situation except reassure him that it was not my son's fault and that his father had problems and could not be with us for various reasons. I am now more open with my son and will answer his questions more directly, as I feel he is more able to understand the situation. He has already worked out that it is unfair that his father doesn't contribute any financial or other support. He is aware of other friends' situations where there is an absent parent and can compare it with his own. But each child's situation will be different and it is a personal judgement how you handle telling them.*

Jennifer *You certainly don't want to ram it down their throats. They will find out or work it out for themselves eventually. They overhear conversations and piece it together .When she was a bit older, my daughter came up to me one day and said something like: "What does unfaithful mean?" or "What does an affair mean?" So we had a long conversation about it because she obviously knew and she needed some* *answers. I told her it's not a good way to behave because it hurts everybody. If you're not happy in a relationship then you've got to do something about it. And even if that means that you end up by splitting up, you've got to be honest. I did also remind her that it wasn't her fault and that we both loved her very much.*

CHAPTER THREE

DIVORCE AND SEPARATION

Mistakes to Avoid, Dos and Don'ts

I'm not a lawyer. I'm not a divorce coach. So why have I become the World's 1st Alternative Divorce Guide? Because I am on the co-parenting journey and I want to share what I'm learning from the many experts I speak to.

I want to bust some myths (like "mediation only works for divorcing parents who get on well"–actually it works for adversarial couples too), and because I was never married so I had no legal rights and HAD to learn how to 'Break up right–please don't fight' *(my middle child came up with that by-line by the way, when he was 10. Thanks for that Joe).*

Why have I created The Alternative Divorce Guide? Quite simply, to inspire and empower parents to co-parent without conflict during or after family breakup.

How?

I take the best resources and people I can find, *add in some non-adversarial legal and mediation experts, shared stories from parents who know how tough the journey can be and the rewards from the life changes it brings – and put them all in a Box. Nicknamed "Divorce in a Box" - you may have read about it in the London Metro or Woman's Weekly, or seen me and my family on Breakfast TV in 2011.*

How do you know who to talk to first *when facing family breakup? You don't. So ask me. I won't charge you. Email me and I'll help steer you towards the people and resources you need NOW (they won't charge for an initial conversation either. You shouldn't have to pay to* find *out how someone can help you, right?)*

Imagine how much easier it will be to agree on a financial *settlement if you are not spending all your money on lawyers' fees, because you are talking to the people with the real expertise–like* financial *planners–who have no* financial *interest in you not coming to an agreement.*

Just imagine how much easier it will be for your children to form healthy relationships in the future, if you act as solid role models of how to deal with a difficult and painful breakup without it turning into a bitter, prolonged court battle?

If you learn things from life, it only seems natural to then share them. Which is why I provide access to free resources via www.alternativedivorceguide.com.

Suzy Miller Alternative Divorce Guide

Spend Less Money on Lawyers:

If you want to know who the right person is to talk to, at the right time, then our Alternative Divorce Organiser will help you to navigate to a better place without wasting money on services you don't need. We help you make the right decisions, save money, and protect your family. Your money is better spent on university fees for your kids than on adversarial lawyers' fees, so to find out what the divorce lawyers don't tell you, register for your complimentary Alternative Divorce Organiser (value £65) right here: It's just a click away:

Registration page: http://startingovershow.co.uk/alternative-divorce-organiser-2/

Elaine I can remember going to see a solicitor. I was just thinking: Right, I've had enough now, I need to get a divorce, and despite the discussions with my husband when I said: "I can't do this any more, I need to leave", he wouldn't have it. So I actually went to a solicitor, feeling very nervous. He was a very nice chap and he basically asked what the grounds were for the divorce. When I mentioned that my husband had been done for drink driving he said: "that's unsociable behaviour, so you've got him on that". At that point I came away and didn't do anything more about it. I think the whole idea of it was too much to deal with then, but I must have gone back to it later and somebody recommended a female solicitor because I had again got to the point where I felt I couldn't put up with the situation any more.

Seeking Legal Advice
by Gemma Hope

The legal issues arising from your separation can appear complicated, confusing and unclear. However, you do not have to deal with these issues alone—that is what lawyers are there for. During a separation you will have enough to deal with so it is important to have a lawyer dealing with the legal aspects of separation for you. Separating from your partner can be a difficult time, there is so much emotional and practical stuff to deal with and the prospect of having to meet with a lawyer can seem extremely daunting.

However, if you have a trusted legal adviser you feel at ease with, they will be there for you every step of the way. They can play a big part in helping to sort out issues involving the care of your children, your home and your finances. A good lawyer who specialises in Family Law will be empathic and highly trained in dealing with emotive and complex family situations and will be able to explain things to you in a way you understand. Contrary to popular belief lawyers aren't all posh, stuffy, fat cats who will make life more difficult for you. There are some lawyers out there, like me, who are down to earth and want to help people through a difficult time in their life in the most positive way possible. Often the first reaction I get from people when I tell them what I do for a living is "That must be a really depressing job dealing with doom, gloom and misery all day" but I don't see it like that. It is actually really rewarding to be able to help and support people through a huge transition in their life and see them move forward.

I always arrange an initial, non-obligatory consultation for potential new clients. As well as being able to gain some understanding into their situation and offer some advice I also see it as an opportunity for people to meet me and see if I am the right kind of lawyer for them. There really is no need to feel embarrassed or uncomfortable about talking about your family problems to a lawyer; we are not there to be judgmental, we are there to help you find solutions and security for your future. You shouldn't feel nervous or intimidated about meeting with a lawyer, but if this is how you are feeling, rest assured many people feel like that. I never underestimate how worried or overwhelmed someone may be feeling when dealing with a lawyer. Whilst at the outset people feel anxious, I have lost track of the number of people who have left an initial consultation with me commenting on how empowered and reassured they feel, and how they wish they had sought some legal advice earlier.

As well as feeling intimidated and anxious about talking through your family issues with a lawyer many people are often concerned about the costs involved. When approaching a lawyer regarding a divorce, for many, the first thing they want to know is "How much will it cost?" And who can blame them? With the media regularly reporting extremely costly divorces among the rich and famous, it is always going to be at the forefront of many people's minds. Unfortunately "How much will it cost?" is, frustratingly, a very difficult question for lawyers to answer exactly. The answer is uncertain and will depend on so many other factors, for example the attitude of your former partner, as it takes two to resolve matters amicably and cost-effectively. A good lawyer will, however, be able to give you a cost estimate and discuss the funding options available to meet your budget.

The best approach to avoid huge legal bills is:

1. Try and keep things as amicable as possible.
2. Be realistic about what you expect to achieve.
3. Instruct an experienced lawyer specialising in Family Law.
4. Give clear instructions to your lawyer and avoid changing your mind or the goalposts if you can.

5. Keep your paperwork as organised as possible. Respond promptly to your lawyer so they don't have to chase you.

6. Give your lawyer as much information and documentation as possible so they don't have to find it for you.

7. Don't use your lawyer for emotional support–ask your lawyer to recommend a divorce coach, therapist or counsellor to help you. Costs aside, it is always important to take a holistic approach when engaging professionals to help you through a separation. I find as a lawyer clients who are having counselling or therapy are in a much better position to deal with the legal and practical side of things otherwise they can get emotionally blindsided and it can prevent them making logical and rational decisions when it comes to dealing with the legal issues.

The sooner you seek legal advice the better, so you can make an informed decision on how best to proceed. The longer you leave it the more potential there is for problems to arise. It is much better to be proactive and avoid problems happening by understanding the legal position from the outset. Many people either avoid dealing with the legal implications of separation or try and deal with it themselves, only to find out further down the line there are significant detrimental consequences.

I have dealt with many cases where I have to try and pick up the pieces after people have tried to "do it themselves". All of them with hindsight wish they had sought some legal advice from the start. For instance one client got divorced online and had thought that this finalised any financial issues between her and her former husband, only to find out years later that her former husband still had a claim on her home and that his creditors were threatening repossession proceedings to recover the monies her former husband owed them. Another client got divorced and reached an agreement with her former partner as to how the matrimonial assets, including a business and properties, be divided up without seeking advice, only to find out further down the line that the agreement reached had left her exposed to significant tax liabilities. There are also incidents where people have not dealt with financial issues, leaving claims open on pensions and inheritance, as well as those where people leave it too late and their former partner has dissipated assets. As far as the children are concerned, an initial agreement with regards to the arrangements for them can sometimes set a precedent for the long term, for example I have dealt with a case where a mum moved out of the family home to go and stay with family abroad for support and left the children at home, only to return a few weeks later to find that the dad was claiming he was now the "main carer" for the children and refused the mum contact and access back into the home. Rest assured it is not at all uncommon for people to see a Family Lawyer for the first time completely unprepared. However, to help put you at ease and to also ensure that you get the most out of any initial consultation with a Family Lawyer it may assist you prior to the meeting, only if you can and feel able, to:

1. Make a list of your major areas of concern.
2. Make a list of questions you want to ask.
3. If you own any property try to get an informal valuation or a rough guide of the value.
4. See if you can find out whether the house is owned by you and your partner jointly or in the sole name of one of you.
5. It is always helpful to know whether there are any mortgages or secured loans and, if so, how much is outstanding.
6. Ascertain the up-to-date value of any savings. Find out the balances of any accounts at your banks and building societies.
7. Get details of any pension schemes.
8. Make a note of your debts e.g. bank overdraft, credit cards, unsecured loans.
9. Make a note of your current net income, including any child benefits or tax credits you may receive.
10. Finally, make a note of the full names, ages, dates of birth of you, your former partner and any children; the date you started to live together with your former partner and (if applicable) the date of your marriage (get hold of your original marriage certificate or a certified copy) and the date of any separation.

In essence, if you haven't already, then have a chat with a specialist Family Lawyer to ensure that the short and long term implications of your separation can be addressed and dealt with so you can move on with your life with certainty, security and stability.

Gemma Hope

Family Law Solicitor at Mayo Wynne Baxter

Gemma specialises in all aspects of Family Law including:

Pre-Nuptial/Pre Registration Agreements, Divorce/Dissolution, The division of matrimonial/civil partnership assets, Prevention/resolution of disputes between cohabitants

Children issues

Gemma is a member of Resolution and a Resolution Accredited Specialist in Advanced Financial Provision and Children Law.

Gemma is a member of and undertakes voluntary work with Brighton and Hove Chamber of Commerce to ensure she is involved with and keeps up to date with the local business community.

Office address: Century House, 15-19 Dyke Road, Brighton, East Sussex, BN1 3FE

T: 01273 223230

Empowerment is everything
by Dawn Tarter

My Story

As a law student many years ago, I suddenly found myself separated and going through divorce. I found myself in unwanted turmoil, financial chaos and emotional upheaval. The worst feeling was the sense that someone else hijacked my life, dismantling it, assuming control over my destiny, leaving me lost and unsure of where to turn and who to trust. I've made many discoveries since then. I learned how to take control, how to empower myself and how to live my true and deep desires. I've become a successful trial attorney, a committed family mediator and a dedicated life coach, each with the same purpose: teaching, encouraging, and transforming you into your empowerment.

As a trial attorney, I quickly realized that the win-lose adversarial outcome of litigation, relying on a disinterested judge's decision, was too often costly and disappointing, feeling unfair for all concerned. I embraced the opportunity to certify as a family mediator and provide mediation services to separating parents here in my community.

Still feeling I had more to contribute, I took an opportunity to master neurolinguistic repatterning and hypnosis techniques. NLP and hypnosis, without medication or therapy, allowed me to overcome chronic major depression and debilitating allergies.

NLP is the perfect solution for me. It's been the solution for so many. I enjoyed it so much I certified as a coach and am now committed to help others achieve their great desires through this empowering process. It has shifted me from solving longstanding problems to creating new levels of achievement, success and wealth.

Best Reasons for Mediation

1. Empowerment.
2. Financial investment in your future.
3. Less stress.
4. Rapid results.
5. You are in control.

The mediator is an impartial facilitator for both parties, balancing the power between the parties, helping them to identify and develop mutually acceptable options. The mediator guides both parties to privately communicate and negotiate with each other for the outcome they want.

Mediation is, in my opinion, the most empowering, satisfying and cost efficient means of maintaining your voice and your control over the outcome of raising your children and successfully moving forward with your life.

The advantage is that mediation is quick, often reaching resolution within hours, and you are in control. On the other hand, litigation can last years, depleting the valuable resources and assets that you are fighting over. That means that with mediation you move forward with your life, the life you truly desire, so much more quickly and with the satisfaction that you determined your own outcome for you and your children.

Don't Make These Mistakes

All too often, the parties coming to me for mediation have not prepared for it. They have misdirected expectations and approach it with a belief that they must each convince me of their arguments. All too often, they presume that mediation will fail if they do not achieve a complete win: eliminating any options for the other parent and gaining all that they demand and more. All too often, they rely on a trial and a judge to vindicate them if they do not "win" at mediation. These mistakes happen because most people argue over the past. If you make these mistakes, your time is not efficiently used to resolve the conflict; rather it is misused to deepen the conflict and to fight.

Think of mediation as an investment in your future. Approaching it prepared with the right strategies, your huge payoff is achieving the outcome you want and a rapid transition into the life you really want.

The Best Strategies for Mediation

Before you begin mediation, act on these recommendations:

1. Be prepared.
2. Know your desired outcome.
3. Have 3 or 4 issues ready to "give up" during negotiations.
4. Fully commit to the best interests of your child(ren).
5. Envision a happy future for yourself.

Transformational Coaching from Conflict Resolution to Your New Life

I'd love to be your mediator. I think it is the most effective and satisfying and healthy process for conflict resolution between 2 people. Hire me instead as your transformational coach. By doing so, you allow me to be your advocate. I come to it with the experience of a litigation attorney, a co-parenting mediator and a transformational coach.

Mediation requires neutrality between parties; as a mediator I coach both parties equally, always encouraging each to focus on the best interests of the children rather than their anger, resentment and vendetta against the co-parent. As your transformational coach, I am your personal empowerment support and my efforts are devoted only to you.

You want your attorney devoted to the legal battlefield. I've personally experienced the devastation of separation and divorce and I've witnessed the unwelcome emotional and financial tolls which my friends and family have paid, many of whom had the best legal representation their money could buy. As an attorney and litigator myself, I highly value legal representation and recommend it for you. S/he can be more effective for you in the courtroom; while your emotional battles are best waged with additional resources and experts such as a coach.

As a transformational coach assisting you through separation, co-parenting and perhaps even divorce, I am devoted to helping you find your core values, your innate empowerment and your true happiness. With NLP and hypnosis, I offer the techniques and skills to hasten your journey through the negative emotions and enhance your positive learnings and outcomes for a more rewarding future.

I am here to guide you through the end of one part of your life and transition you on your journey to the next phase of your life, free of heavy negative emotions such as anger and resentment. I encourage you to focus all of your energy on creating the life you truly desire in wealth, health and relationships.

My Top 5 Secrets to Successful Results from Conflict

Whether you find yourself with your attorney in divorce litigation or you choose mediation to resolve your conflicts, successful results are yours if you:

1. Like Oprah, assemble the most empowering team of experts for you.
2. Think and act clearly. Neutralize the negative emotional charge you feel before you begin the process. (I know: it seems impossible right now; but that is the benefit of techniques from a transformational coach using NLP techniques.)
3. Be resourceful and open minded. (Again: your benefits with an NLP coach.)
4. Control your own outcome.
5. "The best revenge is living well." George Herbert.

Be empowered.

Dawn M. Tarter is an attorney and a mediator, supporting women to reach empowered agreements with their co-parents to raise their children. A Certified Beyond NLP and Hypnosis Master practitioner, she is a transformational coach, helping women to release the old negative patterns

and to embrace the life they desire in wealth, health and relationships. Find out more at www.dawntarterlaw.com and www.dawntartercoaching.com. You are welcome to email her at dtarter@rio-express.net.

CHAPTER FOUR

FINANCES

Keeping Your Head Above Water

Rachel *Worry about finances generally has been a huge challenge and something that if you are in a steady relationship it is possible to share with your partner- "A problem shared etc...." Citizens Advice Bureau is helpful with giving links and contact details of a range of financial advisers and debt organisers who can help. If, like me, you were left with huge debts by your partner, it is useful to know that often if one contacts the creditor it is possible to write these off. If you are divorced clearly you do not take on the responsibility for your ex-partner's debt. There is often help available within organisations such as a welfare fund. My*

employer had an employee assistance bureau which was helpful in receiving 24/7 free practical advice on financial and other issues relating to my situation. Some also offer the opportunity to have counselling by qualified counsellors.

Kayleigh *I'm proud that I found a really good job and that's something that took me a while, but I was able to support myself without getting any child support from my ex, because I didn't get any for quite a while. So I did the financial part of it on my own and made sure that my son had everything he needed.*

Angela *We'd just bought this beautiful house and I just went into panic mode. I phoned my friend who was a carpenter and asked him to come over. There was an unfinished basement in the house with windows and its own entrance. I couldn't lose my house, so I just decided to rent it as a suite (in Canada lots of people have basement suites that they rent out). So he came over and he installed the bathroom, he framed in my downstairs suite for me. I paid a dry-walling guy to come, I actually put the laminate flooring in myself (I don't know how the hell I did it!) then I got a little kitchenette put in there and the plumber came.*

Louise *My biggest challenge was the money (or lack of it!). When things first started to go wrong I was frightened about the lack of money because when you're salaried and life's OK you can't imagine anything worse than, say, having to sign on, but after years of living with my alcoholic husband I knew as a single Mum that I would be able to survive, even if it would be tough. It was really tight but with the benefits I did manage. Over the next few years, if he was doing well, he would at least give me something, though most of the time he didn't have anything, but at least he wasn't trying to dodge it. Seven years after we split up he died of liver failure, brought on by his drinking. Money-wise, I became extremely good and I used to have different pots - one for the gas, one for the electric etc. I also did odd jobs, like taking in ironing or needlework (just general mending, or hems and stuff). It was very tight. One night a good friend of mine (I must have been moaning or something) gave me a present of four cans of lager and I was overjoyed because he knew that my one treat every week was to buy one can of lager. So I made do and mended and bought second hand clothes. The paternal grandmother showed no real interest in the kids apart from sending cheques for* *birthday and Christmas and she would make them out to me, but unfortunately things were so tight, I would use some of the money to buy the kids their presents but then most of it had to go towards bills or whatever it was they 'needed', as opposed to toys or dolls. I did learn to survive and in those days I was incredibly organised; once a month I'd sit down and go through the cheque book and my bank statements etc. This structure helped me not to default on any payments and I didn't go overdrawn, and it also helped me to not worry so much. If you know exactly where you are and when you know exactly where every last penny is going, the structure stops you worrying to a bigger degree, or worrying about the unknown.*

Even if the situation is bad, there's a lot to be said for facing up to it and being brutally honest with yourself and that's your starting point. If you can afford to get good, impartial financial advice this would be advisable at this point in your life, especially as it will help you to plan for your children's future as well as for your own. If you cannot afford to pay for financial advice there are free sources of help for dealing with debt and coping on a small budget. Please see the reference section at the back of the book for contact details.

Louise *There are no frills. There's no: if I spend this now I can make it up next week. Every week has to be boringly organised but at least you know exactly where you are. If everything is on direct debit or standing order then at least you know what spending money you have left –if any– but you have to be in control. They're very hard lessons but you can survive anything that life throws at you as harsh as they are.*

Rachel *Shopping for food can be difficult on a tight budget. You can shop in the evening where there are generally lots of stickered goods. Charity shops can be a real source of cheap, good quality clothes and other items for you and your child/children.*

Angela *He didn't take anything from the house. He said "You saved everything for the house; you got the down-payment together. If it hadn't been for you we wouldn't have had the house." He never really had the mortgage money and also it got him out of having to come up with that money. So he signed papers and signed the house* *completely over to me. We didn't fight about anything. However, I had to pay for everything. I had to pay for drawing up the settlement; I had to pay for the divorce, which finally happened three years ago. I thought that as I'd paid for the settlement, he should pay for the divorce, especially as he was the one getting remarried! He'd never have done it-in fact I probably forced him to get married again because I paid for the divorce!*

Helen *I got no child support from their dad. We were poor but it was fine. You learn how to live within your means. I did a bit of work here and there when the kids were small —nothing major. I did cleaning and ironing, stuff that fitted in with the kids' routine. Routine is very important.*

Andrea *We were lucky, I suppose, because he gave me the house and he always looked after us financially, put my daughter through University and things.*

Elaine *We both needed money to make a fresh start. I had the majority of the proceeds from the house because I had care of the children but he had a reasonable share and of course he just blew it, which was a bit sad.*

Annabel *Then I took over the decision-making for everything at that point. I decided to sell the house, what to sell it for; I put it on the market with the agent. We did have a bit of a wrangle about finances but again in the end I said to him, 2I'm not spending any more money on lawyer's fees. We have to sit here right now and decide what's what and what's fair." In the end he just said OK. Then a load more emotion comes. I had to sell the house which was a project I'd put such a huge amount of emotion into. It was the home I'd always wanted it to be and we'd only just finished it. I absolutely loved that house so much in every way. And then I had to sell it. And I've never actually owned a house since, so I've never been able to do that whole nesting thing, because you can't with a rented house. So I haven't been able to make any house into exactly how I want it to be. I hope I will someday. When I moved up to live with my new husband we rented a house together, so at least I didn't have to live in his marital house he'd shared with his ex. I remember just being in tears for a week during the sale of the house and moving out.We only moved 2 miles down the road because I didn't want to move the children out of their school. The children were at an expensive private school and I had to weigh* up all the pros and cons. I was doing it alone. My ex had lost his job because he was sleeping with a colleague and that was against company policy. I got a certain amount from the divorce settlement but I had to be very careful how I was going to spend that. What I didn't want was to take the children out of school straight away, because I wanted one part of their life to be really stable, to keep the continuity going. All their friends were there. Plus the fact that I have a difficult child, who I felt strongly at the time needed to be in that school because they had all sorts of extra support. My ex was saying "Oh, I don't think they should go to private school," but of course he had a vested interest, he didn't want to put his money into their education. So I did the school fees for three and a half years on my own, out of my money. Now he is at least paying half, but he's doing that instead of paying me alimony, because I wanted it to go towards the school fees. And if I don't start making lots of money soon then they will have to come out of their schools, but I hope that won't be the case. I've set up my own company now. My ex asked me about business the other day and he said to me "I hear you've got your products into Fortnum & Mason's" and he said, "I'm really, really proud of you—I'm so proud of what you've achieved" and I was so angry! I put the phone down and said "How DARE he say that! How dare he be so patronising!" It annoyed me more than anything! He spent two years trying to set up three different businesses, none of which have worked, and now he's gone back to his original career.

Angela I was making lists before he left about what I wanted, I was reading Stuart Wilde about the secret to money is having some, I'd got lists on how I was going to buy a house and flip it, I was saying to myself we had a hundred thousand dollars in the bank when we had nothing – I was into that, and that's the other thing that was hard for him. I had given up the need to struggle, I was not going to be poor; and I always thought it was significant that when we went camping in Oban in Scotland when we first met at twenty, we'd said "We don't care if we're poor as long as we're happy. We can be happy even if we're poor" and I thought, "Why couldn't we have said "we can be happy even if we're rich?"" and that was significant because I had to get an overdraft when we got married, just so we could stay overnight in the hotel for the night of our honeymoon. It was like an indicator right from the beginning! So I'm also working on breaking free from the generational thinking that you've got to be poor to be a good person that the British have so successfully instilled in sections of their society!

Change The Way You Perceive Money
And The Way You Receive Money Will Change
by Wilma Allan

It was a blisteringly hot May afternoon when the lorry backed onto the yard and 4 men jumped out of the cab, meaning business. My heart was racing.

"We've got 2 hours, tops," I told them.

While the sweat trickled down my back I showed them which pieces of my life of the last 8 years were to be packed up and loaded onto the lorry. The last thing to be squeezed in was my old greyhound. He and all my possessions were going to a friend's house, where we would stay until we found somewhere more permanent. The children, who were 3 and 6, were being collected from school and nursery by a friend. We were to meet up and the plan was to re-unite with the children and the 3 of us would go away to the beach for a week while the hubbub died down.

Under the circumstances I wasn't sure how else I could have left. The police had said I was doing a brave thing, leaving. Brave! I wondered, 'How could you stay with someone who, after yet another drinking session, threatens to kill you and then backs it up when he's sober?'

Those events took place in 2005, and as I walked around the supermarket the following day I felt free and alive for the first time in years. I had no idea how I was going to, but I promised myself that I would find a way to become financially independent. I would not be depending on him for anything—I didn't have the heart for squabbling about money. Soon after leaving that relationship, one of my sisters referred to me as a 'single mother', simultaneously loading the phrase with the stigma that often goes hand in hand with that identity. I made the decision then never to think of myself like that. We become who we think we are, and that is our choice, no-one else's—and others will define you by your own definition of yourself.

My parents had not an entrepreneurial gene between them and so no business experience to share. Growing up, life had been middle class and comfortable. Going out to earn money and create an income was an option, but not a necessity. I guessed there would be a steep learning curve, and I was prepared for it, but I had no idea at the time that it would be vertical!

Keeping your head above water as you chart those first months and years on your own is about discovering and standing in your own power with elegance and ease. It's about learning to take complete control and responsibility for all parts of your life–no more blame, guilt or '*shoulds*' for things that are 'happening to you' or 'going wrong'. It's about being willing to learn complete forgiveness–both of yourself, your ex and for those painful events in the past.

Taking control in an elegant and non-dictatorial way also includes taking control of your money. It's possible that you were in a relationship where you handed over the bulk of the financial responsibility to your partner–and so you'll have much to get to grips with. The first thing to realise is that you already have a relationship with money. When you understand your relationship with money you can turn it into a resource that does as *you* want. You become the piper and call the tunes, not the other way around. It sounds simple, I know, but often money problems are as much emotional as they are financial, as I began to find out in 2005.

In 2005 I hadn't worked for money, ie had a 'proper job' for 23 years. Other than a secretarial qualification, I had no qualifications, no training and no experience from the workplace that I could adapt to life creating and running a business. My life experience amounted to 4 years overland travel around the world on a motor-bike, and now 2 failed relationships. I'd been a school bus driver and a ceramic artist. The day I left my second relationship I had been farming sheep for 8 years. So I'm adaptable, resourceful and resilient –which is a great place to start, and I was willing to learn, re-create and adapt.

I was also determined. So, for the first 3 years I bumped around blindly. I knew I wanted to work for myself, and I pursued opportunities with gusto and naivety in equal measure. My first foray into business was network marketing. It was flexible, would fit around the children and I could work from home. It also offered tantalising income potential which had me hooked!

Something that would have stood me in really good stead as I embarked into business would have been knowing what my Money Type was. I only discovered that 4 years down the road, after training as a money coach. This taught me, amongst other things, how to identify money types in others and how to help them maximise their gifts and navigate their weaknesses. It made so much sense, and explained perfectly some of my poorest decisions as I stepped onto my new path. Because network marketing wasn't the golden egg I had hoped it would be, I enrolled on a coaching course to learn how to make network marketing work. Within weeks, my suspicion that I was in the wrong business with the wrong people became crystal clear. So, what had I learned? That coaching was much more interesting and stimulating than network marketing!

The coaching seed had been planted and the kernel grew. So when I saw an advert for a free coaching certification weekend, I signed up for it. I discovered I didn't even know what goal setting was–but no matter, I was hooked.

For the first time in my life, I trained to 'be' something-I had chosen a career. I discovered a passion I never realized I had before. What's more, I also realized I was very good at it–and I began to feel comfortable in what I was doing.

And all the while the fascination with money had been growing. Why do some people always have more money than others, how do some make a mint, lose it and make it again and why do the majority never seem to have enough to make ends meet? I'd begun watching Dragon's Den, The Fixer, The Apprentice–in fact anything where entrepreneurs were helping others out. And what fascinated me was, what was it about people who had made a lot of money–what made them different? Why, when a Dragon had so much in the first place, was it so important to her to make sure that she didn't lose some? Because it did matter, enormously, and in a good way; not in a penny-pinching miserly way, but in a powerful, considered *'How do I get this money I already have to work even harder and better for me?'* kind of way.

I loved that, and that is when the penny began to drop. I wasn't like them then, so why not? What was it about me and my money and my ability to create money that was so different to theirs? If you are in business you are in the business of creating money–right? Of course, I knew I wasn't alone in this phenomenon, but I wanted to find out what made wealth creators so different, how come they were so connected to their money, how come they felt so good about money when so many people don't?

What I realised as I continued my own learning and professional development was that, like so many, I had been totally disconnected to money almost all my life. I had a poor and dysfunctional relationship with money. Because there had never been the necessity to create or earn money, I realized that I didn't know how to! I know it sounds bizarre, how can someone not know how to earn money? I also hadn't realized, early on, that there is no limit to how much money you can create, but, everyone also has an unconscious limit that keeps them at a certain earning level until they take steps to change it. Also, that the more money you create, the more you are able to give back and can do good with.

My curiosity about how people relate to money is my passion, and helping them perceive money differently so that they could receive it more easily became a driving force.

Money is not a bad thing. I realized I was full of my own hang-ups, conditioning, agreements and stories that were holding me back. Whilst being in a position of never having had to earn money may sound great on the surface, the net result was that I was completely disenfranchised with money–totally powerless, able and very willing to give away my power with money at almost every turn. As soon as I began to take total responsibility for all my past money habits, patterns and behaviour things began to change.

Money is a phenomenal coach because it will challenge you every step of the way and help you to grow. This, then, is not just about keeping your head above water. That's the start. It begins with looking at your relationship with money, taking control of your relationship in a powerful way, which means starting to pay more attention to it: where it goes, where it's coming from and the emotions you feel about it.

How you do one thing is how you do everything and money is no exception. Consequently, how you do money is how you do everything, too. You can only continue to be controlled by money or your ex, for that matter, while you are still living with an emotional attachment to either of them. Moving on is inextricably linked to how quickly you can learn to let go of the emotional ties to both money and your ex and, as far as money is concerned, is bound up in the beliefs you have in your ability to earn more. We all want and need money, and there is no shame in that. However, believing that your current income or earning capacity is as good as it gets and all there is, keeps you living in a scarcity mentality which is damaging and unhelpful and will keep you stuck where you are.

Learning to let go of the negative emotional ties to money is courageous and truly liberating. It immediately defuses money as a weapon and gives you the positive control that you need to make powerful decisions that will move you forward.

Creating security and starting to feel good about money is crucial. How you perceive money governs how you receive, so when you change the way you perceive money the way you receive money will change too—it's inevitable. Negative emotions like fear, guilt and shame attached to money only perpetuate a fearful reality with money. I want to give you some steps that will help you to change that immediately. This means regularly stashing some of it away— saving it.

I know saving may not traditionally be the sexiest activity out there, associated with rainy days and scrimping and saving. But what if you could easily create what I call plump cash cushions? You know what each cushion represents and each cushion waits quietly, fattening up in the background, until the time comes when that big oil bill comes up or you've got a major service on the car, or you want to book your family holiday in the sun.

This is the epitome of you taking control of your money. Think of each plump cash cushion as something that will give you peace of mind, security and a deep sense of control, having things taken care of.

Most people don't save because they see the money coming in as already spoken for—it's labelled with someone else's name. Here's the thing. When the money comes in, it's yours. It isn't anyone else's until you decide who you are going to give it to. When you start to pay a small proportion of your income regularly into a cash cushion and then pay the everyday bills, you will start to feel entirely differently about your money.

Saving money in a mindful way, creaming off a little bit consistently before anything goes anywhere else, is the key to making this work—so, pay yourself first!

To avoid living in fear and anxiety a moment longer, here's what I recommend you do.

It's really important to start accumulating and keeping more money because this has a very real and relevant feel-good factor about it. You see, how you feel about your money is vital. When you are fearful, panicky and anxious about money you just perpetuate the cycle you are already in. It's vital to change that mind-set and start to feel good about money, because that is when you will start to notice things changing around you.

Here are 4 steps to help you start creating those plump cash cushions:

Step 1   Decide to start saving and give yourself a date.
Step 2   Open a separate savings account and fund it with a nominal amount—£50 or £100 would be fine.

Step 3   Pay into your cash cushions regularly–at least twice a month. A percentage works well–it's got to be enough so that you start to see something happening and not so much that you leave yourself short on the day-to-day expenses.   5% or 10% is a typical amount.

Step 4   Decide what your saved money is going towards.   I'd suggest no more than 4 cash cushions because it can get complicated.

Money should be enjoyed, and these steps will help you to start taking control of your money and your life immediately. Have fun!

"Change the way you perceive money and the way you receive money will change."

Wilma Allan ("The Money Midwife") is a wealth and money mind-set coach. Her vision, starting with the UK, is to break the taboo about money. It's time to shake things up–to get people really talking and thinking about money in a much more exciting way!

It's time to break the taboo.

Creating and keeping more money is only one part of living a richer life. Wilma has a direct and incisive approach to her work and a mildly maverick approach to life. She makes sure that her clients understand how they relate to money at the outset of any work together. She then goes to work with them to re-align their relationship with money, uncovering those money habits that are tripping them up and breaking through unconscious barriers to creating more income. Wilma also works with clients to overcome more subtle personal blockages to living a successful life.

Wilma works in depth with clients on their individual money type. This gives the client a huge boost and advantage. By knowing which of the 5 money types rules the way a client manages their money, it allows them to optimise their strengths for maximum effect, and they learn how to navigate their challenges. This is a key factor to achieving the success they are looking for.

Through 1:1coaching, group coaching, workshops and public speaking Wilma helps clients to break away from the money habits that are tripping them up and transition elegantly into earning more and keeping more money.

Wilma's qualifications include Money Breakthrough Method Coach ®, Master Practitioner of NLP, Spiritual Master Practitioner and Personal Performance Coach

Wilma lives and works in Monmouthshire, SE Wales

T: 01600 780122

E: welcome@themoneymidwife.com

W: www.TheMoneyMidwife.com

CHAPTER FIVE

CO-PARENTING AFTER DIVORCE

Dealing With Friends and Family
Recreating the Old Relationships
to Suit Your New Life

As a Divorce & Parenting Coach I'm often asked "What is the key to successful co-parenting after divorce?" That's the million dollar question. And while there is no simple answer, I believe most professionals will agree the smartest strategy is learning how to co-parent respectfully. That means remove anger, hostility or vindictiveness from your interactions with your former spouse.

Of course, that's not always easy to do. But it is doable. Learning to hone your communication skills, showing empathy and finding areas of agreement whenever possible go a long way towards diffusing tensions and cooperating as parents. The benefits you derive will more than make up for the sense of satisfaction or ego gratification you get when you hold on to those damaging emotions. Remember, your goal is not to re-establish your adult relationship. It's to become peaceful co-parent of the children you both love!

If you're intent on creating a child-centered divorce that strives for harmony between you and your ex, you need to initiate the conversation and model win-win solutions. If your ex doesn't want to cooperate, that's when your patience will certainly be tested. Look for opportunities to clarify why working together as co-parents as often as possible will create far better outcomes for your children. Over time hopefully your ex will see how much more peaceful the family interactions become when you're not focused on "winning" or butting heads.

In some cases, this just won't work. If your former spouse is totally hostile and unapproachable, you may have to work on your acceptance skills. You'll likely have to let go of the idea that child-centered parenting will occur. At this point, the needs and protection of your children must take precedence over trying to engage your ex.

Sometimes it may be necessary for you to keep the other parent at a distance for the well-being of your children. In other cases it might be your ex who is trying to create the distance from you. These challenges are not easy to resolve, but are certainly worth the effort.

If your extended family is excluded by the less enlightened parent, there are ways to try to work around the situation. If visits have been deterred, encourage your family members to express their love and attention through alternative means: telephone calls, emails, video calls, social networking chats, letters and other creative resources. The key is not to give up. Continue with any means of communication until the family gains access to the children, even if it is a considerable time in the future.

There are no magic wands when one spouse is out to spite or hurt the other through the children. But behaving in the same hurtful way is rarely a viable solution. Focus your energies on discussing the well-being of your children in the short- and long-term. Demonstrate patience and determination while containing feelings of anger and ill will. Should your case need legal action to be resolved, your mature parental behavior will be regarded positively when you're trying to make your case in court. If for no other reason, consider the judge's perspective before you take actions that will reap undesirable consequences.

Don't hesitate to consult professional counselors, mediators, coaches or others who can provide objective guidance on how to restore or create harmony for the sake of your children. Often they can offer perspectives you had not thought of or wanted to consider, which can lead to new options for all concerned. The more open and flexible you are, the better the possibility of turning a difficult situation into a more cooperative one.

Remember, your goal is always what's in the best interest of your children – even when it's not your own first choice. Don't forget, the divorce was a parental decision, not one the children made. Give them a life after divorce that's worth living. When your children are at peace, everyone wins!

Extract from "Coping with Co-Parenting Challenges After Divorce: Keep the Kids in Mind" by Rosalind Sedacca. Get her free e-book on Post-Divorce Parenting: Success Strategies for Getting it Right! At http://www. childcentereddivorce.com

Annabel *Try and be as selfless as possible in terms of the children. That's the biggest thing that's come out of this experience for me, and when I look at relationships that have broken down, so many people bring each other down and it's to the detriment of the entire family because people get vindictive towards each other. That's the one thing that I think women aren't good at: to be able to box up that resentment and put it to one side. Of course it's tough but if you love your children you have to be able to separate what's going on between the two of you and keep it away from them because it's not fair on the children—they didn't ask for it. Whatever your relationship might be and whatever you might think of your ex-partner, the fact is that he's still their father and they don't choose their father. They have to make the best of a bad deal and it must be really horrible for them if they think that they have a parent who is not coming up to their expectations of what a parent should be, and so the more you can help them come to terms with that, the better, and the way is not by being bitter or point-scoring. I also sat down with my ex-husband and said "We should draw a line under what's happened. Whatever my opinion of you, I will keep that to myself and I will never ever slag you off in front of the children and I expect the same from you." And we've kept to that. However irritating he might be I can sound off about him to a girlfriend or my husband in private but not to the kids-because that's just so* *unhelpful to them. So try if you possibly can to make that a cast iron rule. At the end of the day he is still their father and they are a part of him. That's not fair. I'm also a great believer that what goes around comes around and it might take a long time but it does happen: what you do in life comes back to you—good or bad.*

"You've just got to have a sense of respect for the person you have children with. Anger doesn't help anybody. Ultimately you have to say forgiveness is important, and honoring what you had together is important. But it's easy to say and harder to do."

—Nicole Kidman

__Emer__ She's with her dad two nights a week. She was born in Galway in Ireland and I moved over to England when she was four and her dad followed a few months later. We've always tried to keep that relationship as strong as we can. It obviously goes up and down and it can be a bit of a minefield when it comes to ex partners, but he's getting better and better by the year! Even just a couple of years ago I would expect those phone calls saying he'd forgotten to pick her up, those really frustrating simple things where I couldn't depend on him or trust him. But now I'm quite confident that he will remember to pick her up and things like that.

I know the dangers and the pitfalls of allowing yourself to get engulfed in negative thoughts, and I also use that in respect to my daughter's dad. I try and control any issues that I have with him because I know it affects my daughter. So I've worked extremely hard to keep that relationship at a positive level. That's been the most difficult thing, actually—dealing with her dad. He was extremely stubborn and irresponsible for so many years that it was really frustrating for me to try and keep a focus on what was important, which is our daughter and her happiness.

I find it quite sad when I see relationships break down and they're pitting against each other which has a negative effect on the children in the middle. I find it quite hard to control those emotions sometimes but in the end the most important thing is your child's happiness, and you just have to rise above it. So I'm most proud of that. A lot of people around me congratulate me the most part for putting up with some of the bits and pieces in that situation. You know it's worth it now because he's really come through, he's a great dad, he's around, he's friends with all my friends and my daughter absolutely adores him. So it's really worked out. There's also the point that the more negative energy that you hold, the more it eats you up inside and makes you miserable and I always just try and get rid of it because it's not worth it. We've got a nice little apartment together and everyone's happy and healthy. I've dipped in to those pitfalls a couple of times in relation to her dad and in the end I've said: just forget it, and I've put it away. It does mean biting my tongue sometimes but it's much better than feeling that way and having those arguments in your head with an imaginary person in front of you! It's going really well now.

Emer Gillespie is a photographer whose work has been exhibited across the world, including London, Ireland, New York, Paris and Poland. Emer belongs to a group of photographers called "Shifting Perspectives", who are all parents of children with Downs Syndrome. The group supports the Downs Syndrome Association in challenging and changing the perspectives that are currently held in society. Emer's projects include "Picture You, Picture Me" (a collaborative project with her daughter Laoisha) and "Domestication", which shows banal domestic objects captured in simplistic images of beauty and calmness.

http://www.emergillespie.com

Kayleigh *The other thing that I was very strict about (my son and I just talked about this last night) was to make sure not to speak ill of the other parent to my child. I always had faith that in the long run my son would figure it out, that he would know who was there for him, who was not, who was good, bad or whatever. I just had to let him figure out some of the mistakes that his dad made, the choices that he made, the things that his dad was having a hard time with. I just wanted to take care of my son and make sure that we adults kept our issues separate and didn't argue in front of my son or anything. I found that when he was older I was able to be more forthright with him, be a little bit more honest when he asked questions, because I didn't want to lie to him, either. It had to be at an age where he could understand. I always wanted him to know that it was not about him and he was loved by both of us, that his dad just showed it in a different way and that he probably had some rough points in his life where he wasn't able to behave in the way he was supposed to but that was human – we all make mistakes. That was important but sometimes it was difficult, when I wanted to say "Your dad's being a jerk and I don't know why he's not there" but you just can't do that. But he knows now, and now they're talking again and they have a relationship and he's figured it out on his own, so I do feel really* *good about that. I would never want my son to resent me for the things I said about his father–true or not.*

Jennifer *I tried to be brave about letting the children have contact with their father. I know I mustn't be selfish and do what's best for the kids but it was tough at first to let them go, particularly the baby. He was having an affair for all that time when I was pregnant and he sat by my hospital bed and watched me give birth to her, this tiny adorable bundle and then just weeks later he was walking away. She never even had her first Christmas with him – or her first birthday. As they grew older, though, my daughter adapted far more easily to the situation than her brother–after all, she has no memories of us together as a family unit, so there's nothing for her to compare it to. My son really struggled. I remember one time when I dropped the kids off for their weekend with their Dad, he kept saying "Mummy, I don't want you to go". He clung onto my leg and had to be peeled off me. Then he insisted in following me back out to my car and planting a special kiss on the tip of my nose. Turning his little face up to both of us, he simply said: "Why can't we all be together?" Just before and just after weekends with his Dad he became really difficult. He used to dread leaving me and then, having spent time with his Dad, he would play up when he came home because he was missing his Dad. He said" I'm not leaving the kids, I'm leaving you" but how can the children be expected to understand that? My daughter had to write about his family history at school and she wrote "My Dad left when I was born". I can tell you how bad that makes her feel, because she's told me. There was one Father's day when she really struggled to make her Dad a card because she was going through a stage of questioning everything, of thinking: how can he be "the best Dad in the world" if he walked away from me as soon as I was born? She gets on well with her Dad, she loves her Dad and she has accepted the fact of our divorce with her logical brain, but on some level, I worry that those conflicting emotions and feelings are still bubbling away under the surface. When my ex and "the other woman" moved in together he was really keen to show me round the house, and the new family photo they'd had done (with MY children, all in matching outfits-how twee!) I mean really, couldn't he have worked out that might be a bit upsetting for me? He just wants us all to be great mates but it's never going to happen. I'll deal with him because I have to. She'll never be my friend! But what can I tell you? Things gradually get easier. Time heals a lot of things and luckily the children have forgotten a lot of the traumatic moments. The main thing is that both my kids love their Dad and see him on a* regular basis. Whatever I may think of him, he's turned out to be a good father and we can be civil when we see each other for the sake of the children."

Andrea I insisted that my husband took the kids out every Saturday and every time, every single Saturday for years he took them to MacDonald's and they hated it!

Annabel After we moved, we did have a lot of tantrums at the start, especially from my daughter who did a lot of packing her bag and walking to the end of the path. She used to say "I'm going to go and live with a **nice** family!" When we first split up and we moved into this lovely little cottage, their dad only saw them a couple of times. I said to him: "Why aren't you seeing them more?" and he replied "I'm just going to let the dust settle." I was like: "Let the dust settle?! You need to see them NOW!" My daughter never wanted to go with him the first year. She used to scream and hold on to me and not want to go with him. He has a really easy time with the kids because he only has them for two days out of fourteen, so it's really nice for him because he does lovely things with them and then doesn't have to think about them in between times, whereas I do everything, all the admin…he just hugs them and says how beautiful they are and then that's it!

If it **is** you who does the lion's share: try not to worry that your efforts will go unrecognised. Be patient. As your children grow older, a lot of things will become clear to them without the need for you to spell things out. They'll know how hard you worked to make life better for them (and so will you, which also makes all the difference and can give you a warm glow of private satisfaction).

Kayleigh My ex got involved from the very beginning and we ended up going through the courts to get set visitation. For a while it went really well so it was every other weekend and then certain holidays, and then when my son was probably six or seven the visits got fewer and further between. His Dad lived out in the Bay area and I'd moved out here, so I would drive out 70 miles sometimes and he wouldn't be there. So it was heart-wrenching for me, because there were so many times when my son didn't want to go and see his Dad, just because he wanted to stay home, and by the time I'd talked to him and got him calmed down on the way there, then his Dad wouldn't be home and it was hard for me to heal his heart. After some time went by, my son was 9 or 10 years old, he was realising who he could count on and who he *couldn't count on. He made a decision when he got a little bit older, because of the conversations he'd had with his Dad (his Dad would get mad at him for not calling when actually , you know, he's the father, he should be making the effort) and I'd have conversations with him. Little by little–I'd say it was probably for 7 or 8 years-they didn't see each other at all. My son got older and he just didn't want to have anything to do with him any more; he was hurt and angry. He's 26 right now and it was probably 3 years ago that they actually started talking to each other and seeing each other again.*

So they have a different relationship now to the one they would have had, had they been seeing each other and involved in each other's lives all along. I was always encouraging him to talk to his Dad, you know: "It'll be good for you" and then I finally told him: "You know what: it's your choice and I understand. I think it would be really good for you and your dad to be involved. I think it's important, but at this point it's your choice if you don't feel comfortable with that right now. When you do, I'll completely support you." He was maybe 12 or 13 then when he stopped taking the phone calls and just didn't want to know. What I finally realised is that I can't be the mom and the dad. I'm still going to do all the things I can, but the dad is still going to be the dad. I couldn't be everything. I finally let go of "It's not fair" and focused on "Is my son getting everything that he needs from me?" If the answer's "Yes" then I could let go of the "not fair" thing. It was all about taking care of my son and not about whether his dad was getting away with not paying child support, or getting away with just seeing my son when he felt like it.

I'm taking care of my son the best way I know how and I have to be happy with that. I can't control his father. I'm thankful now that they talk and they're close again but it took a while. I think my son's happy now that he's in touch with his dad and I think a big part of it is that my son's got a son of his own, he's going to be a year old next month. Because the mom and him are not together any more I think it's really propelling him, based on his own experience of not having his dad around, to make every effort to see his son, regardless of how hard the mom is on him or how difficult it gets…he is going to be there for his son because he knows how it feels.

Annabel *He was never a particularly good father anyway, even though he'd always said he wanted a family. He was crap when they were babies, he just didn't want to know, he didn't do anything to help and even now he is very happy to take the credit for all the hard work I do! So that's still going on. He's incredibly lazy with* *the children. For instance: he won't pick our son up from school on a Saturday. He makes him sit for two hours by himself and get the bus back every time. It'll all come out in the end and my son will know that his father couldn't be bothered to get in the car and drive for half an hour to pick him up. He just says to me: "Well the thing is, I do this really long drive from London on a Friday night and I do it again on a Monday morning". That's just him all over. He's so selfish; he won't do anything at all unless it suits him.*

__Angela__ He would just do despicable things to my kids: like he would get my middle daughter to go pick up money for him that was owed him and she would take it to him and it was my maintenance money and then he'd give it to other people! So he'd involve her in the whole thing without her realising and she wanted to please her dad. I'd always been hopeful, but he lied and I was always, always hopeful that things would work out, so the challenge was realising that there wasn't going to be "us" again. I had always hoped that we would grow old, have grandchildren together—that sort of thing…After myself, the hardest thing was watching the trauma in my kids.

__Helen__ They only saw him a handful of times for lunch but he never took them off. I wouldn't trust him to take them away. After that it was his choice not to stay in contact. He moved over to India and I think obviously his new wife must have encouraged him to get in touch with his children again and he did. The youngest then wrote back but the eldest didn't want anything to do with him. It never got to him coming over and there were only a handful of letters and then his daughter let us know he'd died. They both had counselling through the school. My eldest went through a rough time through guilt about not having written to him and she ended up needing major counselling. But I asked her the other day if she ever thinks about her dad now and she said "No – my stepdad's more of a dad to me", but the youngest is completely the other way. She's very secretive, very different. I tried to get her to go to counselling again but she won't hear of it. I even tracked the counsellor down that she'd had at primary school. We had one visit and my daughter said "No–I can't do it any more", and yet the counsellor said that she definitely needed to do more counselling, so what can you do? Maybe she'll start again when she's older, when she's ready. They also worked with a bereavement charity called Winston's Wish, which was brilliant. I was the odd one out in the group, the only parent there who wasn't *actually grieving, although I was there to support the girls. After that, my eldest went on and did some fundraising for them.*

Louise *I had taken the kids down to the station to meet their dad, because he was going to have them for the day. I parked the car and he started walking towards the car and I knew instantly that he was drunk. My son was already out of the car, very excited to see his father, and my daughter was just getting out, and I just said to them "Kids: get back into the car right now." Of course they were completely confused because their father was "walking" towards them. So, I got them in the car and I put the windows up and then I walked round and told him exactly what I thought of him, and of course they were completely bemused. Up until then I had made the decision (I don't know whether it was right or not) that they wouldn't know the details, but this instant I knew I had to tell them and explain- especially as they were so disappointed. So I took them into town and bought myself a coffee and them an ice cream and I started to explain. "The problem with Dad today is ... " This then developed into a conversation of why things had happened over the years, in words they could understand. I did use the word 'alcoholic' and my daughter needed that explained (they both did, but my son was too young to even question the word). So she said: "Oh that explains it!" So she had known all along that there was a reason, that there was something wrong—she just hadn't known exactly what it was. We must have sat and talked about it for about an hour and conversations have gone on since then about it and how it affected us. They saw him a couple of times more after that and then it all went quiet. After a few more weeks I found out he was in hospital and that was when he died (of liver failure due to his drinking). I suppose it was quite a good thing that they had seen him like that and we'd had the conversation, because in a way it prepared them for his death and gave them something to tell the world about what had happened, what was wrong with him. Both my children have turned out to be lovely people—caring and—on the surface-stable. I say on the surface because my daughter has hidden a lot of stuff about her father which, as she's got older, has bubbled to the surface. She's dealing with that now. But I remain concerned about my daughter; she's far more fragile than she lets on.*

Angela *I think men are different. I've read somewhere about that cut-off mechanism (because they went out to hunt or they went off to war) and they don't have the same attachment. My husband had coached my kids' soccer, their baseball; he'd* *been involved in their upbringing. My youngest daughter was shocked because she'd always been his baby and we'd just had my niece's birthday party, where she'd been sitting on his knee at the Dairy Queen and when he left, literally, he left everybody. I mean my sister and her kids never saw him again until years later when they bumped into him shopping. All our friends, all the people who'd supported him: he just cut them out of his life. He divorced everybody!*

The guilt got in the way of his relationship with his kids until he finally realised that they all loved him anyway and he could take that in. One of my daughters was at a kind of school they have here in Canada which is self-directed. They have learning guides and a teacher tutor who watches the whole class and makes sure that everyone is progressing properly. I was able to go up and talk to the counsellor at the school and explain the situation, but what happened with this daughter is that she became completely insular. So we wanted her to go to a counsellor but she wouldn't go. She still hasn't really opened up to anyone apart from herself and her journals. She'd gone back into a state of depression about a month ago, so she went back on her medication and she went to see her brother and they had a really long visit. I said to him: "Do you think she pulled away from you when Dad left?" And he told me: "When Dad left I would go and sit on the end of her bed and try and talk to her and she would just pull the covers over her head and curl up in a ball, so I just decided I should step back and leave her alone."

My son started to behave differently. He had a really tight circle of friends and they were so concerned about him not being honest with his emotions, like they were used to him being, that they actually went to the counsellors at their school, who called me. They had my son in and talked with him because they were worried about his mental health.

Now the kids accept him for who he is. They totally understand his limitations: everything has a "but" to it, so if they go over there, they've suddenly got to go off in his truck and do this... there's always a condition attached to everything. So they really love him for who he is but they don't have any major expectations.

Louise *There've been a few things with my daughter where she has come to me because something was worrying her. Once she wrote me a letter and put it on my pillow because she wasn't too sure how to verbalise it, because it was something that was so painful and embarrassing for her and I read it and I understood immediately that she needed help. It was a physical thing and so I took her to the doctor's and got* *it sorted, after which we discussed it and it went away. I remember at the time one of my friends saying to me "Thank God that you've got that kind of relationship where nothing is out of bounds to talk about." With my son this is not so evident! When I ask him questions sometimes about what happened at a party or something, he says to me: "I'm not talking about this to you. This is the sort of conversation to have with a father!" and I say, "Well as you haven't got a father, I am your mother and your father so you'll have to talk to me!" but he's more shy, especially about things like that! Having said that, however, my daughter's been away at University for five months now and my relationship with him is getting better and better. He's chattier with me more now that he's not being overshadowed by his sister. And it's actually really nice.*

At some stages, depending what's going on in your life, you can often find that you develop an extra closeness with your child, which is something to treasure and build on. If, on the other hand, you are finding it tough to get through to your child or teenager there is help at hand. One very useful thing could be to learn how to develop optimum rapport. There are some wonderful NLP techniques for this. Please visit my website **www.thelifeyoudeserve.co.uk** to order your free factsheet, "Communicating with Children, Talking to Teens". There are some things that your child may not feel at all comfortable discussing with you and in that case I can heartily recommend an excellent website for them to explore: **http://www.doctorwellgood.com** is streetwise enough to have teen appeal, yet offers excellent guidance on staying safe and healthy.

Angela It's hard I think for Moms when they're struggling themselves to even see clearly what is going on. I think it's really hard to be objective when you're going through that grieving process yourself, you know? Everyone does the best they can, you just do the best you can do at the time, right? Forgive yourself!

As single mums it's easy to fall into the trap of thinking you're not good enough, you haven't done the right thing. But the fact that you were there, you cared and you noticed, that has to count for such a lot, and as they get older your kids will recognise that.

Angela Even six months later, nine months later I would sometimes say "Perhaps we'll get back together" and my son said "Don't you dare!" They all saw how emotionally manipulative he was–not just to me, but to them. Friends started coming over more. My son just blossomed into this individual personality, he got a black hat, he just became really free to be who he was and I didn't realise that that joking kind of "put down" humour that the British sometimes have, how that had been impacting my kids' lives. So in one respect it was better for everybody.

My son pulled back and had nothing to do with his Dad at the time he left, so that's why I think he's now allowed to go to his stepmother's house–because he wasn't there right at the beginning. Whereas my youngest daughter really wanted the connection, so she'd go over and stay there, but of course she was depressed and down and her stepmother just thought she was sulking! I mean: go figure–you're in your Dad's new girlfriend's house and you're feeling down! And even to this day, my daughter has always tried to visit and stay in touch with her dad but his new wife has rejected her, and although my son can go and stay, my daughter's not welcome. So she won't have her over now.

I wanted to protect my kids and the hardest thing I had to learn from the counsellor was that they had a relationship with their Dad and I could not protect them because he had "fired" me in my relationship with him. And that's the hardest thing when you're a mum, to watch your kids suffer. All of the kids are really very philosophical. So I talk about forgiveness with all of them but everyone is different, they all handle it in a different way. Now, if he's ever invited to any of the kids' houses, they wait for him to actually phone and say he's on his way before they actually expect him. Because he really isn't a man you can trust to be there when he says he's going to be there.

Even if you may wish at times never to lay eyes on them again, experts agree that children benefit from continuity and continued contact with your ex and his family, providing that there is no risk to you or the children (as in the case of an abusive past relationship). Indeed, if you are prepared to get past that awkward stage after your initial split, where everybody struggles to know how best to behave or what best to say, you can now begin to create new relationships which will be a positive help to you in the weeks, months and years to come. Undoubtedly there will be bitterness and disagreement between you. Believe me, I understand only too well how difficult it can be to remain on cordial terms, both now and in the future, but it's up to you to be adult about it and you can have the inner satisfaction of knowing that you are doing the right thing by the children. A good thing to bear in mind is that you can choose to avoid conversations about the past or your split by merely choosing to concentrate on conversations or arrangements pertaining to the children. This way they can continue to play a loving and positive part in your child's upbringing.

When my husband first left and the news got out I was absolutely inundated with other people's opinions. I spent almost every evening on the phone once the kids were in bed, talking to well-meaning friends and family members. It got to the point where I developed a crick in my neck from having the phone clamped to my ear—a sort of "repetitive phone injury"! Not only did everyone have their own view about why this previously unthinkable thing had happened, they also wanted to give me advice on how to handle it. Naturally, I was very touched that they cared enough to want to share their thoughts but some of their advice was confusing, contradictory or downright unhelpful. One relative told me that I must "pick myself up, dust myself off and *concentrate on developing my career*", something that was far from my mind as I was totally immersed in looking after my tiny baby and three year old son, trying to find somewhere to live and dealing with divorce proceedings! I waited with bated breath to hear the advice of a wise old lady who had, herself, been left with two small children but was non-plussed when she simply said: "You've got such a beautiful speaking voice, you should apply for a job as a newsreader with the BBC!" In the end I decided to let it all wash over me. Only *you* know how it was in your marriage or relationship – nobody looking in from the outside will ever have the same insight that you do about why things went wrong. Read all the books, talk to others who have been through similar situations, speak to unbiased professionals about it and in time you may gain valuable insights as to what caused the disintegration of your relationship. Be prepared to realise that you may never know for sure why it all went wrong but that the things you have learned will guide you in the future and can prevent unwanted patterns resurfacing in other relationships. You can find details on my website* of therapists and counsellors for one-to-one help including a fabulous offer of a **FREE SESSION** with a local NLP and Hypnosis practitioner.

When my husband first left, members of his family (or mutual friends we'd had as a couple) with whom I had previously been very close became conspicuous in their absence. It took me a while to understand that for many people the easiest way to deal with awkwardness, embarrassment or shame is just to blank the situation completely. It's a form of denial, if you like. Try not to take this personally and, instead of concentrating on friends and family who are unwilling or unable to be present in your life at the moment, focus on the ones who *are* present and seem willing to offer help and support, especially if it's of a practical nature, such as an offer to babysit or help out with some household maintenance.

With some people that you spent time with as a couple it will be relatively easy to pick up a relationship again, albeit a new one where your ex no longer plays a part. With others this process may be less successful. It may be that they have taken sides (or you would prefer them to take your side). Or perhaps the strain on you both of trying not to refer to your split or talk about your ex all the time will prove impossible. In my experience, reliving the painful details in this context and with a person who may already have divided loyalties, leaves you feeling aggrieved and unhappy and stirs up a lot of emotions-for both parties. I found at times that it was a little like losing a tooth–try as you might to stop it, your tongue keeps finding its way back to the gap and exploring the hole where the tooth once grew. Sometimes the best decision for your happiness and peace of mind is to respectfully go your separate ways.

This is a time in your life when you should be open to finding comfort and support in the most unexpected ways and places. I discovered a trick for getting through the days when I felt so miserable I could barely put one foot in front of the other. It's hard to look into a totally uncharted future without panicking or feeling morbid, let alone deal with the endless daily slog of bringing up small children single-handedly. What helped me was to pick a thought or mantra to repeat to myself throughout the day. Something like "What doesn't kill you makes you stronger", or "Into every life some rain must fall". This might sound corny, but it really works. I use inspirational thoughts and sayings on a daily basis even now and I find it can change my whole day for the better.

"Expect trouble as an inevitable part of life and repeat to yourself, the most comforting words of all; this, too, shall pass."

—Ann Landers

"The word "happiness" would lose its meaning if it were not balanced by sadness."

—Carl Jung

"Just do what must be done. This may not be happiness, but it is greatness."

—George Bernard Shaw

"Happiness is your own treasure because it lies within you."

—Prem Rawat

I learnt through my counsellor that the grieving process has several phases. The sadness I had no problem with–I must have cried for England by now–but the anger bit I found really hard. I have always been brought up to be polite, not to rant and rave and to keep hold of my temper. It was quite a revelation for me to be given permission to express my anger but once I got the hang of it, boy did I get mad! I spent two whole days consumed with incandescent rage and it felt so good! I discovered some great ways to deal with all this anger, too. Tempting though it was, I did not resort to a slanging match with "the other woman". Instead I sat down and wrote her the pithiest, most brutally honest letter. I held nothing back. I poured all my feelings of bitterness, jealousy, betrayal and scorn into that letter. It took me two hours to write and I was absolutely howling by the end, tears streaming down my face. I slept like a baby that night and in the morning I reread it and put it somewhere safe. I never got around to sending it. On the other hand, I found that laughter was an even better medicine for me. Some money came through after a commission I'd completed some months earlier and I decided to treat myself to a much-needed mini holiday at a local health spa. Once I'd dropped the kids off with my mum I booked in to this peaceful oasis and made the most of the rest, relaxation, soothing treatments and healthy food. I also made an unexpected discovery, when I met three other women there, all of whom were recovering from relationship traumas. One lady had just discovered that her husband had an illegitimate love child, by then aged four. Another had finally plucked up the courage to leave a violent partner. The last of the group had just discovered that after having three children her husband had completely lost interest in her and wanted a divorce. They were all clever, confident working women–one a barrister, the second a manager in a large accountancy firm and the third a personal trainer. It just shows you that life has some tough lessons for us all and we are none of us exempt, however perfect or organised our lives might seem to the outside world. We christened ourselves

"The First Wives Club" after the film of that name. One thing I've discovered about being plunged into the depths of misery is that it teaches you to make the most of every minute and to grab happiness and laughter where you can. We had one hilarious dinner where (much to the horror of any fellow diners who might have been eavesdropping), we sat and fantasised about committing the perfect crime to avenge ourselves. She of the unfaithful husband had already started to exact her revenge. The poor man was being forced to grovel daily. So far he had paid for her spa visit, redecorated the whole house and had booked an expensive holiday in Florida in an attempt to make amends! The other revenge scenarios sound very cruel in the cold light of day (though we cried with laughter at the time) and all involved a gruesome yet particularly ingenious and appropriate murder—let the punishment fit the crime, we reasoned!

Recognise that it's perfectly natural to vent your negative emotions. As long as you are not actually hurting yourself or others, my advice is to exorcise this negativity in fun or creative ways. I had a lot of fun ripping up or carefully cutting up photos of my ex (don't worry: I kept the best ones to give to the kids one day!) It felt surprisingly liberating to light a small bonfire in my back garden and burn these, along with an old tie of his! A good friend of mine cut a jagged line between her and her husband in one of their wedding photos, stuck the two halves on a card and made it into a wedding card for her cheating ex-husband and his new bride-to-be. The message inside read: "Wishing you all the happiness you deserve on your wedding day"… now whilst this might not fit into the calm and forgiving category, I bet it made her feel good at the time!

It doesn't have to be all doom and gloom, though! Make sure to put into practice your new sociable single girl status every once in a while and remember to have fun. I reasoned that even though I was too broke to get a babysitter I would still enjoy my friends' company every now and then. It is true that I was usually too knackered to even contemplate those prepare-in-advance dinner party menus. However, I figured that my friends knew me well enough to perch on a kitchen stool and chat to me whilst I prepared our meal. And if I hadn't had time to dust, well hey, I just turned the lights down low and lit a few candles; nobody was any the wiser. I remember one such occasion well. I managed to get the children tucked up in bed and fast asleep by the time my friends arrived. Whilst getting ready, I gave myself a stern talking to. I reminded myself that people said that I was intelligent and bubbly and even quite witty on occasion.

But of course when you have been passed over for a younger independent single woman with her own car and flat and you are struggling to wipe baby sick off your shoulder it's hard to convince anyone, least of all yourself, that you are good company and quite a catch really. I decide that all I could do was to try to hold my head up high, look as gorgeous as possible under the rather trying circumstances and hope that someone would see through my tired and somewhat frazzled exterior to the sophisticated and sexy woman that I hoped might still be lurking somewhere underneath. Anyway, that particular night was fun. Nobody minded that we didn't eat dinner till ten–the food was delicious and we talked and laughed well into the night. When they had all gone I felt a sudden surge of happiness, bubbling up from under all that grief. I lit some new candles, turned the music up high and danced. I danced for the unexpected joy to be found in passages of sorrow, for the future and for the person I knew I really was. My dance was an affirmation–a mad, giddy moment where I forgot my despair and renewed my faith in myself. If someone were to ask me what the biggest surprise was in my situation I would reply that when you have been down as low as a person can go without giving up altogether, only then can you truly appreciate those precious moments of happiness that arrive from nowhere. Only then can you truly live in the present and fully make the most of the "ups" that come your way.

> "Live by this credo: have a little laugh at life and look around you for happiness instead of sadness. Laughter has always brought me out of unhappy situations."
>
> —Red Skelton

> "Happiness often sneaks in through a door you didn't know you left open."
>
> —John Barrymore

Emer No man is an island, to use a clichéd phrase. Every single person should have some kind of support network. In my case I wasn't exactly very successful in making friends with other parents here and that's something that if I have another child I will work harder at, because then I was just so busy. I was working and studying and I was just kind of dropping and running to work, or up to London to study. So I didn't have that luxury of stopping for coffee or spending time with the other parents. I would hope that might change next time. I would like it if my photography takes off a bit more and I don't have to work full time. I still had a network of friends but none of them had kids, but I was still able to join them for barbecues or meet them down the beach with my daughter. So she's been surrounded by adults her entire life and I think that really helped with her development and ability to communicate, and she's kind of like the child of the big friends group here, which is really lovely to see when we meet up down the beach or go on day trips to the farm and stuff. So I think it's also part of the whole thing that I know there are different situations out there, but there is always a lot worse out there. If you're a parent it's important to keep your head above water for both you and your child

We still do have adventures, though–I mean, my daughter's been all around the world including Australia and Thailand and all around Europe. We still go on adventures: we're going to Iceland on Thursday. It might be a bit different when I have a child with my husband but I always know that my Mum's around–she's flying over for her birthday and her other Granny's coming over because we're going to Iceland and we've got that great family and friend support system that allows us to do those little adventures, which is really great. I think I'm quite lucky to have that.

Louise *The children were very small. My daughter had just started nursery school and my son was even younger. I was always very rigid about routines because when you're on your own, even though it would be very easy to just go with the moment, I think children do need a routine. Bedtime was always a certain time and later, when I started doing my college degree, it was always incredibly important to me to have them in bed before I started studying. When you're a single parent you also need those hours to yourself, just to be quiet, if nothing else. Children, especially small ones, are so noisy! That would also be my time to talk to adults. I would put them to bed, come down and make a phone call; I would talk to somebody adult, otherwise life was all "child speak"! It was quite important for my sanity. Apart from anything else, you can feel very isolated when you are a single parent and you need that social element to bounce off others, or to ask for advice, or help or support- otherwise you can feel very isolated and then you get out less and less and less.*

Andrea *My friends were all gobsmacked, absolutely gobsmacked because we were the most unlikely couple to split up. My older sister was furious! I've mostly drifted* *away from our joint friends we had at the time. After a while the invitations just stopped coming; but then a lot of them were his friends, I suppose, so they still see him. But my friends were brilliant, especially my friends at work when I finally went back, and my neighbour looked after me too. You just want to keep talking and talking about it and crying on everyone's shoulder and probably boring the pants off everybody! But it helped me.*

__Angela__ When it first happens and you feel like you've been thrown on the heap, don't believe yourself when you're telling yourself "Nobody wants to hear my story". You feel like: "I can't talk to my friends, because who wants to hear this story?" Or: "How can I possibly go and talk to them about this __again, all this stuff that's going on__?" You feel like you're a burden to friends almost because of what you're going through. But really good friends don't care—they just want to be there for you as much as they can, so don't isolate yourself just because you feel that nobody wants to have you around! It's a terrible feeling. That's sort of a thing women do to themselves, especially if they have been mothers and wives and have been raised to please people, they don't want to burden anyone. You're not really burdening, your opportunity to heal is just being expanded.

__Annabel__ You absolutely have to be able to share it with someone. They don't even need to have been through it themselves. You just need to be able to sit down over a glass of wine and say "Life is crap." I used to end up laughing, just laughing hysterically. You have to see the funny side of things. Use your energy positively. "Poor me" becomes a self-fulfilling prophecy.

It seems to me, from all the stories that I've listened to, that being able to share our experiences is a real gift that women have. One of our best skills is the ability to talk through our feelings, which is an ability that a lot of men don't have (or perhaps are uncomfortable to explore).

__Emer__ I think the most important thing I learned was that if I hadn't allowed myself to regain my individuality coming out of that relationship I wouldn't have been as happy a parent, which then reflects on the child. I think my daughter's amazingly happy and positive personality has benefitted from my ability to turn a negative into a positive. We created this lovely, happy home in Galway for years where we always had *an open door to everyone. I think most of my friends have lived on my couch for two or three months out of their lives, because we always had that welcoming household, which I think is important. Yes, you're a mum but you're also **you** and if you're not happy then the family isn't happy.*

Rachel *Taking care of your appearance gives you more confidence and a boost.*

My many years as an image consultant, colour and style coach have taught me that women who, like you, have gone through a major change in their lives benefit hugely from getting professional advice on the best way to present themselves. This is the new you, does your appearance give out the messages that you want the world to hear? Looking great is a wonderful way to feel better and also to be treated with more respect. It's also liberating and life-affirming at this point in your life to take stock of how you look and to assess your wardrobe. What do your clothes say about you? 'Victim' or 'Force to be reckoned with?' 'Elegant and stylish' or 'Tired and past it'? I'm using humour here to make my point, but you get my drift. Finding out the colours and styles that flatter you most will make you look more attractive, make your clothes look more expensive and also save you a great deal of money because there will be no more mistakes hanging in the wardrobe and each time you buy an item, it will co-ordinate and team up with all the other clothes in your wardrobe. You'll need far less clothes but you'll have tons more to wear! The way you look can help you to express your personality, have a lot more fun and enhance your standing and reputation—not only amongst your friends, colleagues and the community but also in the eyes of your children. Paying attention to your personal grooming will ensure that never again will you be embarrassed when an unexpected visitor calls or (worst of all) you bump into your ex! Going for a new job or going out on a date will no longer prompt that dreaded quandary of "Help-what am I going to wear?!" Send me an email (**vivienne@thelifeyoudeserve.co.uk**) to ask for more details, help and advice.

Never underestimate the power of a support network. This can be made up of people you know, friends and family, single parenting experts or others in the same boat as you. These days there are so many fantastic resources that can give you the help, advice and inspiration just when you need it. For a free email newsletter delivered straight to your inbox every month packed with articles, tips, advice and offers, go to my website* and fill in your details. As to how to deal with the daily grind of your new life as a single mother? Be kind to yourself. Take the advice of people you know if it helps, and ignore it if it doesn't. Trust your instincts. I also found that when I was feeling at my most vulnerable, some people in my life made me feel safe and comforted and some people made everything feel worse. Pay careful attention to who these people are in your life. You owe it to yourself (and your sanity) to minimise your exposure to people who bring you down at the moment.

"Happiness is not a brilliant climax to years of grim struggle and anxiety. It is a long succession of little decisions simply to be happy in the moment."

—J. Donald Walters

Louise Over the years, word spread that I "had got most T shirts" (you know—"been there, done that, got the T shirt!"), that I had experienced A to Z, and I would get so many people turning up with their problems because I understood. Because when you have been there, and been through it, I think that's when you can give solid advice.

Renowned parenting expert Sue Atkins shares some invaluable tips:

Retaining healthy relationships, wherever possible, will help to reduce the stress all round in the family, and in particular when dealing with the "ex." Regardless of the quality of your relationship with your former partner, you are now responsible for bringing up your child jointly, but separately.

So grab a piece of paper and a coffee and ask yourself:

- *How do you work through key issues with your ex-partner*
- *What guidelines, do you both lay down and how consistent, are you both?*
- *Do you agree on bedtimes, pocket money, sweets, homework, computer time or when they get older, boyfriend/girlfriend time?*
- *What are the benefits, if you did?*
- *Are you ever tempted to buy favour with your child? What are the messages they receive from you doing this?*

Positive Parent Top Tip

Remember, children need a consistent approach from both parents.

Children are very good at picking up vibes from their parents. They're very sensitive to our moods. If we can explain to our children, why we're feeling anxious it will help them to understand and they may not be so worried by our behaviour. For example," I'm sorry, I am a bit tense today, as I've just had the phone bill in."

It's much easier for a child to handle something specific, rather than to just see you in tears or in tantrums! Also, some children always assume it is their fault, and it's good for your children to know that they are not the problem.

- *How do you speak about your ex in front of your child?*
- *What important message, are you sending to your child about their father or their mother?*
- *How do you think your child feels about seeing their parent criticised?*
- *Have you considered that your child might still miss their estranged mum or dad – regardless of how you feel?*
- *How do you cope with your feelings toward your ex?*

All by myself.

It is easy to underestimate the complex tensions that accompany divorce-even a fairly amicable one. Your child may be angry and upset because one of his parents has left, but as you're the only parent around for him to vent his feelings on he is likely to take it out on you. Your child may become sullen and awkward or loud and angry. It's very hard for you on top of everything else that you have to cope with. However, try not to take it personally. Try to understand your child's feelings of dislocation and try and take a positive view.

- *How do you allow your child to express themselves, however negative the emotion?*
- *What ways do you allow your child to let go of hurt feelings and resentment?*
- *How do you handle the anger and accusations? Do you argue back? Leave it until she's calm down, and in a more receptive mood? Talk it through rationally?*
- *What are the benefits, if you took a step back and distanced yourself from the emotion? Would you feel more in control?*

- *What are the long-term disadvantages to "slagging off" your ex-partner. How might this damage your relationship with your child?*
- *Will it help if you didn't see it as a competition?*

Positive Parent Top Tip.
Forgiveness is the key to moving on.

Maintaining civility.
However bitter you may feel toward your ex, however hard you may find it to forgive, think about the benefits of maintaining a degree of civility with them. You will not be able to control what your ex-partner does or says but you can control your own actions. If your partner continues to use your children as pawns, your best move is to refuse to play chess! The greatest temptation, particularly if your partner is behaving obnoxiously, is to return like with like.

But what are you teaching your children?

Guidelines for your children.
It can be a lonely and confusing place for children during this difficult time. Just like bereavement, healing is not linear. So it can take however long it takes!

Here are some Positive Parent Top Tips that have been drawn from the experience of mums and dads who have had broken relationships.

1. *If at all possible, be positive about your ex-partner. At the very least, try not to be negative. Tell your child that you both of you love him.*
2. *Don't criticise your ex to your children-keep in mind that it's their mum or dad you're talking about. Remember, your child feels loyalty to both.*
3. *Leave photos of the missing parent around, use their name-it helps your child heal.*
    It's important that your ex is still part of your child's life. Be ready to talk naturally about the good things that happened. It will help your child move easily through change.
4. *Encourage your child to keep in contact with the non-resident parent through e-mails or phone calls. Show respect by sending them a birthday card.*
5. *Try to encourage your child to see her mum or dad. Try to encourage the relationship, or at least keep the doors open for better things to come.*

6. *Don't use your child as a messenger or a spy.*

7. *Discuss with your ex about Christmas, weekends, and who's going to have who and when. And stick to the arrangement if at all possible. Children need stability in their lives.*

8. *Encourage your child to continue their relationship with their other parent. There will always be long-term issues to work out and face and the quicker that they do that the easier it will become.*

9. *Remember it's important to keep your promises to your child. He may feel let down by one or both of his parents so only make promises to him that you can keep.*

10. *Keep on reassuring your child that the breakup is nothing to do with her- especially if your child continues to seem anxious about it. It's important that your child doesn't blame herself.*

Another difficult area when relationships break down concerns the "in-laws."

The only thing to suggest is that you do the right thing for your child. Even if it's not what you would want to happen. Seeing and being in contact with the in-laws may be an unpleasant or painful experience for you, but they are still a very relevant part of your child's family, their culture, and their heritage. It is healthy for your child to have a sense of family that includes all relatives.

Healthy relationships, including those with the ex, need to be worked out. Success doesn't happen overnight, and often calls for much personal sacrifice and self-discipline. But it's worth all the effort in order to provide a stable environment for your children so they can grow up to be happy, confident and well-balanced adults

Stay centred and grounded – remember you are doing your best and pat yourself on the back!

Sue Atkins is an internationally recognised Parenting Expert, Broadcaster, Speaker and Author of the Amazon best-selling books "Parenting Made Easy – How To Raise Happy Children" & "Raising Happy Children for Dummies" one in the famous black and yellow series, as well as author of the highly acclaimed Parenting Made Easy CDs. She has just launched the 1st in her series of Parenting Made Easy apps for iPhones and iPads.

Sue offers practical guidance for bringing up happy, confident, well behaved children from toddler to teen & specialises in using The One Page Profile Process with families to boost long term self esteem & self confidence.

She regularly appears on the award winning flagship ITV show "This Morning", BBC Breakfast and The Jeremy Vine Show on BBC Radio 2 and is the parenting expert for many BBC Radio Stations around the UK. She has a regular monthly parenting phone- in on BBC Surrey & Sussex and her parenting articles are published all over the world.

To receive her free ebooks bursting with practical tips and helpful advice from toddler to teen log on to www.theSueAtkins.com and download them instantly today.

CHAPTER SIX

STAYING FIT AND HEALTHY AND KEEPING YOUR ENERGY LEVELS HIGH.

Creating Happy Memories That Your Family Will Treasure

Building Your Support Network

"Being a mom has made me so tired. And so happy."

—Tina Fey

A wise woman recognizes when her life is out of balance and summons the courage to act to correct it, she knows the meaning of true generosity, happiness is the reward for a life lived in harmony, with a courage and grace.

—Suze Orman

You owe it to yourself and your children to stay fit and healthy. As you have no doubt discovered by now, looking after kids can be exhausting! Increasing your level of fitness will give you the renewed vitality and energy to keep up with all the daily challenges of parenting. It is worth bearing in mind that choosing to make just small changes in your daily life can dramatically improve your wellbeing.

It may be that getting an unbroken night's sleep is a distant memory but there may be ways to catch up on some sleep with the help of a friend or relative who can pop in for an hour or a local teenager that you know and trust to be sensible who is keen to have some babysitting experience. You may feel nervous about doing this to start with but if they come whilst you are still in the house (albeit having a much-needed rest in your room) then you can rest assured that they will wake you up if they need to. If, however, you are in the enviable position of having children that sleep through the night, make it a priority to get a good night's sleep (tempting though it may be to stay up late on the computer, reading or watching late night television). Six or seven hours a night can help keep your blood sugar balanced.

Eating a healthy diet is also essential both to maintain your ideal weight but also to boost energy levels. We all know about the downside of the sugar rush—the sugar low you get afterwards. Eating too many high carbohydrate-rich or processed foods, or consuming too many sugary drinks or foods can leave you feeling sleepy, sluggish and downhearted. Most of us single Mums have succumbed to comfort eating at some point and the occasional treat is perfectly fine but take it from me, it makes you feel so much worse in the long run and you can get onto a slippery slope which is hard to get off. Before you take a bite, ask yourself first: am I actually thirsty, instead of hungry? How will this feel as it slides into my stomach – not just now but for the rest of the day? Will eating it make both my body and mind feel good in the long run? If the answer is no, consider working out which emotion is eating you, step away from the food and spend a little time paying attention to nourishing your soul and spirit instead. For more advice on my eating strategies of naturally slim people, visit my website.

Exercise releases endorphins, those wonderful feel-good chemicals, and who doesn't enjoy some feel good factor floating around their bloodstream? It may be an effort at first if you haven't got the fitness bug already but hang on in there. You'll find that it's an upward spiral – the more you move, the more energy you have and the more enthusiasm to exercise and so on…what methods you actually choose are up to you, but here are some ideas:

The key is to fit exercise into your daily routine. If you do this, you are much more likely to stick to those good habits. After a while you will grow to enjoy both the experience and the results so much that if you have a day without exercise you'll really miss it. Every bit of time and effort counts and you don't have to carve out an hour or more for a gym workout if that proves too much of a challenge. Walking is perfect–it's free and fresh air is good for both you and your child. A 15 minute brisk walk will burn around 100 calories and this could be pushing a pram or buggy or walking to the park or the playground with an older child. Sometimes, as every mother knows, a walk can be a less than positive experience if your child is having a bad day, but you can use lots of little tricks to make the journey fun. Playing I Spy can often work, or looking out for and counting specific things along the way–flowers, trees, feathers, leaves or pebbles or even first one to spot 3 red cars, or two taxis: make it up as you go along! Once children are old enough to accompany you on a bike or push their scooter they'll enjoy it even more. Of course if you can tie your walk in with an activity or special mission (allowing your child to post a very important letter in the post box, walking to the park for a picnic or a game of football or going to the shop for an ice lolly) they will feel much more motivated. By building a regular walk into your family routine you are not only benefitting yourself but instilling in your children healthy habits that will serve them well in future life.

Of course if you have a garden there are tons of activities you and the kids can enjoy, such as trampolining, badminton, or kicking or throwing a ball about. Swimming is another excellent way to stay active. At first it might seem quite a performance, especially with small children on your own. Getting yourself and them undressed and into swimming gear, bundling their clothes into a locker and then dealing with floats, armbands and anything else you may have brought. I used to find when my boys were small that I got quite cold standing in the shallow end but we soon developed a favourite game where I held them safe and bounced along the bottom of the pool with them. It may look stupid but as long as they are having fun and you're getting some exercise, who cares? Another popular trick with my sons from about aged four onwards was to get them to hold onto my swimsuit straps and tow them along, pretending to be a pony. Once it's time to go home it can sometimes get a bit fraught whilst you get everyone showered and dressed (especially if one of them is a toddler intent on escaping for its own little adventure) but you soon get into a routine and again, getting your children used to the water and teaching them how to swim and stay safe around water is vital. Gardening is a good way to get healthy fresh air and exercise and children often love being involved with age-appropriate jobs, from watering or planting seeds for the littlies to building a bonfire, painting the garden fence, raking or even mowing the lawns for the older ones. Pocket money may be a good incentive to motivate teenagers but if you have brought them up to regularly participate in chores around the house this may not be necessary.

If you don't feel like going out for a walk when it's wet or cold outside think about exercise you can do inside. When my two boys got especially boisterous in the evening we had a ritual where I'd pick each one up in turn and dance like crazy round the sitting room. We had a favourite song we'd play and it was a great way for them to burn off some steam. Judging by how out of breath I got, it was great aerobic exercise for me too! Speaking of dancing, this is something you can have fun with and it's such a great way to use up some calories. Line up your favourite tracks and dance round your sitting room like no one's watching! This works equally well with or without children, so enjoy on a regular basis. I have a plastic exercise step (available at retailers such as ebay and Amazon for a reasonable price). To get me started in the morning I line up a great playlist of my favourite music and do step exercises. Depending how much time I have at my disposal I can fill up a few minutes this way or take half an hour if there's time. Don't forget to warm up and cool down properly. For more ideas on fun ways to get and stay fit for all the family, visit my website and order your free fact sheet.

Rachel Although it may not sound an attractive proposition, getting up early on a Sunday to go to a rugby match in the winter or a cricket match in the summer, it can be helpful to join your son at a local club. Not only is the exercise good for them but the fresh air, the opportunity to meet new people and a change of scenery can be beneficial for you too. I think interaction is really important with others and going outside and meeting up with friends, colleague and acquaintances is usually a positive thing and normalizes your situation. You may even find your situation is not that bad after all compared to others!

Put your oxygen mask on first!
by Jonathan Roche

When you fly, the safety presentation always talks about putting your own oxygen mask on prior to you helping your kids. This also relates to your health and your kids' health. You need to take care of yourself and be as healthy as possible to be able to do the best job taking care of your kids.

Honestly, think about this for a minute. Skipping breakfast, not having healthy snacks during the morning and afternoon, not staying hydrated, not working out, etc. do not put you in the best spot to be your best you!

Parents often put themselves last, even sacrificing their health and wellness because they want to be good parents. They care so much about their kids that they put all their focus and energy into them. However, parents are at their best when they take care of themselves. Invest some of your valued time and energy in yourself. Put your oxygen mask on first and it will pay off many times over for your kids.

Your team is following your lead!

Even when we want to take care of ourselves, staying consistent with workouts and healthy eating is hard work! Our negative voices are constantly hitting us with excuses to blow off our workouts and eat badly. When this happens, I invite you to focus on how much your family (especially kids if you are a parent) follows your lead!

The only real way to help your kids get health and to a healthy weight is to lead by example. Trying to force exercise or tight nutrition on kids usually backfires.

According to The American Academy of Child & Adolescent Psychiatry:

- *A child with one obese parent is 50% likely to become an obese adult.*
- *A child with two obese parents is 80% likely to become an obese adult.*

A parent's weight and lifestyle has a large effect on their child's activity level, eating habits, and outlook on weight. So take the stairs instead of the elevator, park in the furthest spot at the grocery store and do something active with your kids each day so that you can fit a little exercise into your lives.

In simple terms: You have to walk the talk as far as living and being healthy!

There are many positive qualities that you work hard to pass on to your children: treating people correctly, a strong work ethic, studying, doing the right thing, etc. But sadly and unfortunately, most people also pass on their health and weight problems. If the idea of having tons of energy and being healthy isn't enough to get you "in the game", then get healthy so that your children have a chance to be healthy adults and to someday tell stories to their grandchildren or even great-grandchildren.

Our kids become us! If we are active and healthy they are active and healthy. Unfortunately, the opposite is true. Your negative voice will try to talk you out of the following statement but it is a fact: You are your family's Chief Wellness Officer! Wear that hat proudly and hit the gas. Your kids will become healthy and thriving adults if you help them build healthy habits now!

Give, give, give, give, etc

If you are a Mom, then you spend every waking moment giving. You are taking care of the kids, the house, the meals – the everything. You are the glue that keeps the house together.

At one point in your life you and your health were a top priority. Maybe it was in high school or college or more than likely it was before your first child was born. Moms are the hardest working people on this earth and you are also the first ones to remove yourself from your own priority list.

You need and deserve to do something uncomfortable: You have to stop giving and start taking. You deserve to carve out personal time each day to exercise (even 10 minutes is fantastic!) and invest in your health. Your house won't fall down and your kids will end up benefiting from a more energized, healthy, and happy version of you.

You tell yourself you don't have time so you put your workouts or your health off for another day. Then the days become weeks then become months and then become years. I invite you right now to not only put yourself back on your priority list but to move your health and your workouts up to the top (yes, I am serious). Yes, in the near term your kids may gripe but in the coming weeks they will see the positive changes in your energy and mood. Then everyone wins!

So carve out some "me time" each day and you will be pleasantly surprised how much better you feel (mentally and physically) and how much this benefits your family.

Thanks to all of you Moms for keeping our families functioning. You are all Rock Stars!

Treat yourself as well as you treat your kids!

How well do you treat yourself versus how you treat your kids? Would you ever let your kids skip meals, drink limited water throughout the day, avoid physical activity for weeks or months at a time, not eat anything for 5 or 6 straight hours, etc.? Honestly, think about this for a minute.

You deserve to treat yourself as well as you treat your kids! Your health is too important not to do this. Consider it an investment in yourself. Plus, by taking time to invest in your health each day you will bring more energy to your kids and serve as an example of health and fitness for them to follow.

You and your health are worth it!

Waiting for the Ideal time is a dream

Most people keep telling themselves the same type of stories:
When things settle down at work I will lose the weight.
When the kids are older it will be easier to focus on myself.
When I invest in a gym membership I will start getting fit.
When things are less stressful I will start eating right.

You get the point. The sad thing is that when we wait for the ideal time to start losing weight and getting fit it rarely comes.

Our lives are perpetually busy and crazy (especially for Moms) and we need to ditch the dream that a magical day in the not-too-far future will happen when everything will line up and we can go for it! If you wait for that day you will be waiting forever and you will continue to be robbed of becoming who you deserve to be. Stop putting it off and go for it right now!

extract taken from "The No Excuses Diet: The Anti-Diet Approach to Crank up your Energy & Weight Loss!" by Jonathan Roche; available on.Amazon.com

Jonathan Roche is an Award-Winning Fitness Expert, 18-time Boston Marathon Finisher (running 17 times for the Dana-Farber Cancer Institute – where his Mom was treated), 12-time Ironman Triathlon Finisher and is the author of "The No Excuses Diet: The Anti-Diet Approach to Crank up your Energy & Weight Loss!"

Jonathan weighed 224 pounds and was wearing size 38 pants in 1995 when his father (who was obese) died of a cardiac arrest. Jonathan has kept 40 pounds off since 1995 and he wants you be the next Success Story! Visit www.NoExcusesWorkouts.com to join the Free No Excuses Team.

Rachel Going out to the park to meet friends is something which we could enjoy together, however cold it might be. Spending time with your child doing different things is always worthwhile. I found encouraging my son's love of sport, art and writing has paid dividends. When I have been able to I have taken him to the cinema, museums and the theatre.

Elaine At the end of the day, as long as the children are happy so is the parent, so whatever keeps the kids happy, you're willing to do.

Kayleigh I think that with my son's dad only being around sporadically, he was able to spend a lot of time with my parents and my family. Creating those memories was wonderful, especially now that my dad isn't around any more. My dad, mom and my son had their annual camping trip and sometimes I would go along, sometimes I wouldn't, but he just loved it, he looked forward to that the whole year and had such a good time. We spent a lot of time with my family and that was hard to do sometimes because of the distance and co-ordinating schedules, but I really made an effort to make that happen, and I of course enjoyed that time with my family too. I made sure to recognise what his passions and talents were—you know: baseball, karate, he got into a couple of different things. He was really interested in art, he still loves to draw, so I made sure that he took classes at the community centre and gave him the space to draw and the tools; he loved being outdoors so I would take him to the caverns near here and you could go inside the caves and look at all the things in there, animals, the zoo—just spending that time with him and taking lots of pictures. We'd get irritated with my mom sometimes because it was always another picture and another picture. After a while it got really tiring, but my mom taught me that and it turns out that now I always have my camera or my phone and you get to look back and relive those memories. So now with my grandson, I'm making sure that my son and I are taking lots of pictures so I'm passing that down too. When my son got a little bit older we would go out to breakfast on a couple of Saturday each month and he would have to put all these quarters into the machine to get the toy, and that was a little tradition. Christmas was always with my family so we'd get in the car the night before and he'd have the same tradition that I had growing up, so the room with the Christmas tree in would be closed off and Santa would be in there with the cookies and the glass of milk and he wouldn't be able to see until we were all up and they would draw the curtain back to the family room and then we would all go in. At Easter he would colour in his Easter egg and then he'd have to go look for his Easter basket, so those were some of the holiday traditions that we had.

You, too, can become the keeper of the family heritage. However tiring it is to do all this yourself, building family traditions for you and your child will ensure that you both have a treasure box of memories to delight in. Rituals and traditions are such a huge part of every culture and a great source of comfort and joy for people of all ages. Life may not have turned out as you expected, you may not have a conventional family (whatever that may be these days) but you can start creating that rich and colourful family history, those wonderful family traditions right where you are now. You'll be glad you did, and so will your child. And don't forget to make a record of it in some way. The photos or videos will bring it all back and provide a talking point for years to come.

Kayleigh Between the ages of 12 to about 20 was a kind of dark period for my son and at 17, when my dad became ill, I was spending so much time away from home with my dad that I really had no idea what was going on in my own home or with my son. We talked about that dark period recently and we also look at all the videos and pictures from before and he says "I was really happy back then." He saw the pictures and the smiles and that really brought it all back. He's struggled since then and still does now as an adult with depression. He's learning to cope and I help him too with his anxiety but he can look at those pictures and remember he was that happy person, and continue to strive for that happiness. I know he will be happy again. He knows we had a lot of good times and there'll be more to come too, and I feel good about that, that I was able to give him that.

Louise I was also diagnosed with reactive arthritis. Friends and family were vital. The children were 4 and 6. When you are a single mum you don't lose your old friends but you do find yourself banding together with other women who are in the same situation. When I first became ill it was through friends and family that I managed to cope because I was completely incapacitated. My daughter became a little mother. I managed to get them ready for school and do their packed lunch and that would be it. Other people would give them a lift to school and pick them up; my mum was coming over and cooking meals. I got slightly better in the February and I had been told by the hospital this would happen after about three months, but I then had a major relapse and was given the choice of hospital or bed rest, at which point my mum moved in. So again I survived with the help of others. You also find out who your real friends are. Some people who I thought would be helpful or understanding weren't, and then I found out I had amazing support from unexpected people and that was a very interesting discovery. One of my first goals was to be able to pick them up from school myself, so it was an absolutely massive milestone. There was a day that my mum drove me to the school and I was able to walk in, incredibly slowly and then sit on the steps and wait for them, and the look of joy on the children's faces because they'd become so used to me not being there! Eventually I was able to walk to the school on my own.

Being the sole carer for your children when dealing with a debilitating handicap or health condition can, in fact, provide an extra incentive to becoming more mobile or fighting to improve your health by taking those small steps towards your goals. Women, and in particular mothers, can achieve so much when they are striving–not just for themselves, but for the sake of providing a better situation for their children.

Louise There were various goals along the way. The other one was to do a walk that I used to do with them before I became ill. It's about a mile and a half and includes climbing up and down a hill, on uneven ground. It took me about three years to be able to walk it again. It was a November day and I had the children with me and it was just amazing, albeit we had to have lots of stops along the way for me to sit down. That was massive for me. As time went on I was able to manage with less outside help, but I also learnt that if I did too much then I would pay, so I used to do a little, and then stop. My reliance on friends became less. Also-and I *don't know whether this is a bad thing or a good thing-the kids became a lot more self-sufficient from quite a young age. I remember being quite astounded when people would say about their children "Oh ___ can't stay overnight because they're afraid of going anywhere strange or without me." whereas my kids were used to being farmed out here, there and everywhere without a backward glance from them, without a moment's complaint, with a smile on their faces. So I couldn't understand this clinginess that other kids had, that some mums perpetuated.*

I also remember that my children spent time with relatives or trusted child minders–this was a necessity for me if I was to be able to work and have some sort of a life outside my main job as mother. The big benefit was that as a result my children were far less clingy, they were used to socialising with other children and adults and as a result (and judging from the feedback I got) were therefore a pleasure for other people to spend time with. However hard it was for me to send them off sometimes, it was also good preparation for school trips. I still remember when the day arrived for my son's five day outward bound adventure with his class. For some of his classmates, it was the first time that they had ever been away from home for this length of time (or indeed, in some cases, ever). I spotted a huddle of tearful mothers- distraught at the prospect of losing their little cherubs for four or five nights and completely losing sight of the fact that they were meant to be going off to have fun-which of course had set off their children, some of whom were themselves now wailing! Whilst I sympathised, I was glad to instead be able to give my son a big hug and a cheery wave to send him on his way, secure in the knowledge that I would not have contributed to any potential homesickness on his part. And sure enough, he wasn't even remotely homesick, had a whale of a time away from home and came back full of stories about his exciting adventures. Because my children were so used to staying away from home, they were able to have far more fun and embrace the whole experience, as was I.

Louise *Through the circumstances my kids became a lot more resilient and sociable. I do think independence is a huge benefit. Now that they're older, not only are my two going off and doing work experience, but where I work I have quite a lot of other work experience kids coming in and you can tell the ones that have had no life skills in this area compared to the ones that have. And it's amazing how they* *approach the tasks that they're given. We had one girl and she hadn't got a clue what to do with the Hoover—she'd never had to use one, as a chore or to help out, and she was completely without a clue. From an early age my two had to help out around the house. My daughter did take on this mother role far too early and this is a role that she has carried on to this day. This is something that I regret but it was a combination of her character and our circumstances. Even my son helped with gardening and painting the house. Again, one of the biggest benefits of being a single mum with children is that for us, we became a team. We would have board meetings where we'd sit round the table and we would discuss things that were coming up, what to do about it and this continues today. I very rarely do anything without discussing it with them. Another little memory was dinner time: always sitting at the table, eating the evening meal together. Not so much now that they're older, but certainly when they were younger, we switched off the television and sat down and talked about the day, which I believe is really important.*

I have a similar policy in my house and I also found Stephen Covey's book **The 7 Habits of Highly Effective Families** (published by Franklin Covey) extremely helpful and inspiring, so I instituted his suggestion of family meetings in my house. There are some wonderful ideas and imaginative activities and exercises here for building rapport and trust within the family, creating and living by core family values and teaching children how to work as a team, prioritise and develop into productive and considerate members—not just of the family unit but of society as a whole. It certainly helped me a lot, to discover what was really important to me in being a parent and think about the kind of example I was setting to my children. Without wishing to sound melodramatic, I still maintain that being a parent is the most important job I will ever hold and it's something I am continually evaluating and working on—and I'm sure that process will carry on until I die.

CHAPTER SEVEN

ONGOING SUPPORT FOR THE CHILDREN

Dealing With Their Grief and Their Behaviour When They "Act Out"

What They Are Going Through

Rules and Values

School Plays and Holidays

As I sit down to write this chapter I have a memory, a little snapshot of the days when I first became a single Mum. My son's teacher spoke to me about something that he'd forgotten to do (or rather *I'd* forgotten to get him to do, as he was still quite small then and couldn't be expected to take responsibility for his learning–something that he does so brilliantly these days). Anyway, she wasn't cross or anything, just giving me a gentle reminder. That was the week when I was coming to terms with the news that the children had already met my husband's new partner. I was the last to know about the meeting and I was just distraught about it at the time. The minute the teacher finished speaking I discovered to my horror that tears were welling up and before I could stop myself, I started sobbing. I'm sure the poor woman couldn't work out what she'd said to provoke this flood of emotion! She was very sweet and sat me down on one of the tiny children's chairs and gave me a tissue and ten minutes to calm myself down. Throughout their time at school I always informed the boys' teachers of any issues at home so that they could be aware and keep a special eye out for any behaviour that would indicate they needed a bit of help and understanding with everything they were going through. They've always been so good at school and I didn't want them to get told off for not behaving normally or not concentrating when they had such a good reason to be "below par". It was embarrassing at first to admit that ours wasn't a standard happy family but then, with the divorce rates being what they are these days, I realised that ours would also not be an isolated case.

Kayleigh *I don't know if it was because of things going on with his father, but my son was a really strong-willed child and I do remember there were times when he didn't want to go to day care and then there were times when he didn't want to leave! There was one time that I was just so tired and I still remember this so clearly. He just started throwing a fit and he was crying. He was little, about 5 years old, and I broke down. The day care director took me to one side and put her arm around me. I was at my wits' end, I think–there was just so much going on, just normal stuff, just mom stuff. It was so nice of her to do that, though. My son did start giving me problems with his behaviour and not doing his homework for school around 11 or 12. That was the time that he decided not to see his dad any more, so it must have been linked but at the time I didn't realise that. I was just trying to hang on, making calls to the teachers, helping him with his homework and making sure he stayed on track, but looking back it's kind of ironic that that was the time he started getting into a little bit of trouble with homework, talking in school and things like that. So it definitely had an impact on him. He did start going through a depression, where I actually got him going to counselling. You know, he didn't really talk about his dad much. I don't know what they talked about in their sessions but his dad didn't seem to be the centre of it. I do think the situation with his dad had a lot to do with it, The biggest mistake that I made was over-compensating with things to make him happy for that moment. But it continued on and that's when I go away from what I thought my true parenting skills were, you know—being so diligent about making sure that he had his chores and making sure that he appreciated money. I think at that time I was so tired that I started falling away from what I really believed I should be doing as a parent, and that's when I just started spending the money on him. It would make him happy and then that would make me feel so happy but then 2, 3 weeks later he'd start again and he'd want something else to make him feel better. Of course he was just a kid and he didn't realise that it was just a Band-Aid, and it's not going to make it better in the long run. I knew that too but I think it was just easier to do. I don't think I was trying to take the easy way out but I was tired and that became the new normal for me, just to hand things over like that. So at this point even now he's struggling with the value of a dollar and how to balance his cheque book, and I 'm trying to help him be good with his money and to help him realise that it's not a free ride- you don't just stick your hand out and someone gives you something. So that's something I look back on and really wish that I'd reached out to someone and gotten help sooner or stopped it early on. I guess fathers do the similar things. My son's dad has certainly done that. He doesn't want to be the disciplinarian, he doesn't want to be the bad guy—he only sees him for a limited time. I guess we learn from our experiences and at least I get to talk to my son about how not to be tempted to make the same mistakes with my grandson!*

"I learned a lot from my Mom. My favorite lesson: remember there is no such thing as a certain way to parent and to remember that you are learning along with your child-it's ok to make mistakes."

—Regina King

It's so hard, isn't it, to know the right path to tread? So many single mums find that this uncertainty about how to deal with both discipline and also worrying behaviour in their children only adds to the stresses and strains they are already facing.

Angela I went to the bank. One of the parents of one of the kids I was teaching came to say hi, and I was so distraught that she thought one of my kids had died because I was incoherent. I had 3 months off work because I couldn't function. I was just on the floor. So all I did was hold it together to get that room downstairs finished and get a renter in there. I'd pretty much paid for everything there myself anyway. The kids got me through. I went to counselling that was provided by my employers. They were telling me to do stuff for myself, and that was hard because really I'd been a mum for 26 years, married for 30 years and doing something for myself was such a foreign concept for me! My son, sadly, stepped in as the man of the house. He sort of became my protector, which was a really unfortunate thing at his age to be feeling he had to do. Then my eldest daughter turned 16 that August and her Dad didn't acknowledge it at all, didn't even send her a card. My ex was in a breakdown situation himself, so I'm not blaming him, he was operating in survival mode; we had been faithful as far as I know, so it was a big thing for him to leave. He told me he felt like his head was going to explode, or that's what he told me. So he was in his own personal torment.

Divorce, like life, is rarely neat and packaged. This is especially true for divorcing parents. The reality of divorce comes with unexpected twists, constant frustrations and times of utter helplessness when children act up or pull away.

Here are three tips for coping with times when your children are venting, lashing out or expressing their own frustrations about being caught up in a family adjusting to separation or divorce:

Diffusing blame. Some children, especially pre-teens and teens, may blame one parent or the other for the divorce. Sometimes they may be correct in this interpretation, given circumstances they have been aware of for years (alcoholism, absent parent, domestic violence, etc.). Other times they side with one parent as a result of their prior relationship dynamics with that parent. Regardless of why you or your spouse is being blamed, keep your cool. In many cases blaming is a defence against feeling overwhelmed by the circumstances in your child's life. Suddenly there are so many changes in such a short period of time. Often this behavior is not meant against you personally. It is merely a child's way of coping. When you keep this in *mind it is easier to not personalize the outbursts and accusations. Patiently remind your child that you understand their frustrations. Acknowledge they have a sincere right to feel that way. Tell them how much you love them and how much you regret their hurt and pain. Let them know this was a difficult decision for both parents yet one you feel is the best alternative for your family's future happiness and well-being. Be patient and consistent. And don't internalize a child's expressions of frustration as a lack of love for you as a parent.*

Countering distress. Often, negative comments from your children are expressions of distress and not criticism. Children want and need encouragement, support, and security during times of stress and change. If their needs are not being met because one or both parents are too caught up in their own hurt and drama, it is not surprising to hear negative comments and outbursts. When you realize that this is a call for attention, recognition and the emotional healing that you can provide, you can move into action. This is the time to reinforce your comments about the key messages every child needs to hear. They include: You are safe. You are loved by Mom and Dad. You will not lose Mom or Dad. You are not to blame for the divorce. Although change can be challenging, everything will work out okay.

Patient acceptance. In many ways divorce is like death. Sometimes the best thing you can do is fully be there for your children and understand what they are going through from their perspective. Talk if they want to talk. Hug and cuddle if they respond to affection. Continue as many family routine activities as possible on a day-to-day basis. Be honest and sincere when you are upset or frustrated by changes in your family life-and let them express their frustrations, as well. Most importantly, accept and acknowledge whatever they share with you as okay for them to feel. Try to put yourself into the mind-set of your six, ten or fifteen year old and experience the world from their viewpoint. It will help you be more empathic, less judgmental and more open to really "hearing" what they have to say.

Extract from: "When Children of Divorce Act Out – Caring Parents Step Up!" by Rosalind Sedacca

Sometimes children will express their feelings in unusual ways and an experienced teacher will have the wisdom and intuition to recognise this. I still remember doing some volunteering at the school and being amazed at what children said on occasion. I once heard one little boy (whose father, I knew for a fact, had died) solemnly tell two classmates that his father had an important engineering job in China and that's why he never got to see him. Of course, there may be repercussions in the playground, too. Children who are frightened, angry or upset might become more aggressive than usual because anger is a common part of the grieving process, especially for a child who has no way of controlling a situation that his or her parents are responsible for and who has had no say in the way the situation is handled, such as where he or she now lives, how often they see their absent parent– if at all and other matters. Change is tough for everyone to get used to, most especially for children. It's also possible that your child may be teased because the sad fact is that other kids may use any personal information to get the upper hand. I still remember my son being told by another boy "My Dad loves me, unlike your Dad! You don't even live with your Dad and he doesn't care about you." Ironically, this other boy had a very difficult relationship with his own father-whom he didn't live with-so perhaps he, in turn, was acting out his own feelings about that. But at the time my son was devastated. He rushed home, spoke to me and then rang both his biological dad *and* his stepfather (both of whom care about him very much) for reassurance. The two boys had a serious talk with their form teacher; they have put it behind them and are now good friends.

It's true, I remember someone saying to me: you'll never know how much of an effect the split has had on your child, because you won't be able to compare it to anything.

Families that are dealing with divorce or separation need to pay particular attention to conscious disciplining. Children forced to handle the break-up of their family dynamic may be holding on to a broad range of feelings and thoughts that need to be expressed, accepted and influenced in a positive direction. I encourage parents to seek out the assistance of a counselor or other professional as soon as they sense any depression or other problem behaviors. This is not a time to forego discipline, which is an essential part of the parenting process. It is a time to pay keen attention to your children to make sure they are moving through the challenges of "change" in their lives with age-appropriate acceptance and behaviors that fall within a normal range for your family.

Extract from "Disciplining Children through Divorce: Limit their Behavior but Not their Thoughts" by Rosalind Sedacca

Emer *So far we haven't had behavioural problems, although it is getting more and more difficult watching the gap grow between her and her peers and also thinking about what's going to happen when she's eighteen. I want her to live independently, I want her to get a job —we talk about it all the time. So my main goal is to instil that.*

"My mom has made it possible for me to be who I am. Our family is everything. Her greatest skill was encouraging me to find my own person and own independence."

— Charlize Theron

Jennifer *I remember having a really hard time coping with my son, who took to venting his anger and grief on me or our poor dog, who came in for some violent kicks or smacks when I wasn't looking.*

Helen *I wasn't the strictest mother going! I can remember being really frazzled, especially at bedtime—oh my goodness! And prising them out of the car to go to school…I foster kids now and I've got far more techniques I use now to cope with all that. I'm armed with them now! With the little boy I'm looking after now, if he goes into a mood, kicks out or gets abusive I will walk away (as long as he's safe, that is). I say "Come to me when you're ready and you can apologise". There's no point in trying to reason with someone who's having a tantrum like that. I'm a table person for meals, not in front of the TV. I didn't really have any set policies about things. I was just there for the kids, always there for them. We've always talked about stuff. They're both teenagers now and I'm trying to talk to them about contraception at the moment and they're like "Aaargh!" I've tried talking to them in the car but they always have headphones in! I can't do it at the table because we're mixed ages with the little boy I'm caring for and it's not appropriate. But I'll keep going: it's important.*

Kayleigh *As a child I was very shy and always labelled as such. I began to think that it was very negative, so I was also very careful not to put any labels on my son. I would talk about his behaviour but not label him as a particular type of person. I always felt very strongly about that because it'd had such a strong impact on me, and my mom didn't do that to be hurtful to me, she was kind of trying to push me. I remember that was a big struggle and I ended up doing all sorts of things that a shy person wouldn't normally be expected to do, like being a cheerleader or trying out for the band, just to break away from that! In the end, it did propel me to have experiences I normally wouldn't have had, but it took years to get away from being 'the shy one' and to not feel like it was a bad thing. Comment on behaviour, don't label the child. You know, we're all making mistakes as we go. There's no instruction book on trying to be the perfect parent. But when you hear real stories from other parents, that's really comforting because you know that I'm going to be OK, my child's going to be OK.*

* **Andrea** I remember one of the most difficult things when it first happened was dealing with homework and stuff. My son was in junior school at the time and he was asking me questions about science, things his dad would normally have helped with. I phoned my ex up and asked him to help a couple of times. I remember when my son was a teenager; one night he was so late back, it was the middle of the night and I was really, really worried, so I rang my ex up and he kept dithering and saying "Oh, what shall I do?" and in the end I said "I don't f***ing care what you do, just sit there and worry, like I am!" and slammed the phone down! There were a few occasions like that.*

* **Louise** I think you have to develop some kind of warning signal. My daughter used to laugh, because she could instantly read my face and know when I was cross or upset or annoyed, and then she'd turn to her brother and say "No. Stop what you're doing and look at The Face!" Even now, she does it. But you have to save your energy for the big battles. Say a child is aged seven and does something really stupid, that really makes you very cross, you can't expend too much energy on that one thing because it's probably small in comparison with what's to come. If they tune out your voice at a young age you will have absolutely no effect on them when you really need to, especially when they get older. I had one friend who used to go off all the time and now her children completely ignore her, whereas because I very rarely really have all guns blazing... when I do, it's very noticeable and they take note. I have a DVD of after one of the children's joint birthday parties when they were little. I'm filming, so I'm not in the picture at all, but they have to open the card first and then the present. My son is only just four and he's so excited, he's just bursting with excitement and he can't wait to rip the wrapping paper off the present and my daughter's not far behind. But I hear my voice, quite low, saying to my son: "No, open the card first. Wait your*

turn, it's your sister's turn first." and he does as he's told and I was quite surprised, but there it is on tape. We had our family rules. Even now, we do things our own way and there's a security in that because everyone knows what's expected.

Establishing your values and rules as a family is crucial. I remember having an awful row when my second husband completely lost the plot and started yelling and swearing at me. It was Father's Day (ironically) and I scooped up the kids and a picnic of whatever I could find, and a rug and swimming things and took them to the beach. In those days the best thing was to get out of the house, just get away from him and as we were unloading our stuff from the car one of the boys said to me "Why did he swear, because we don't swear, Mummy, in our house, do we?" and I replied "No. You're absolutely right, because that's one of our rules- we may know how to swear but we don't swear at each other." We had a really good discussion then about how he had different rules when he was growing up and that was one of his problems and I was able to say to them that no one had ever taught him to respect women. So I carried on and said "I want you to know that when you grow up and you have a wife or a girlfriend, it's really important to treat them kindly and with respect." So we had a really good conversation and actually that's what I remember most about that day, rather than being yelled at and being incredibly upset at having to spend the day by myself with the boys rather than the Father's Day outing I'd originally planned. Because actually, once we got onto the beach it was gorgeous sunshine and we had a lovely, peaceful day. I loved the way that they already had a very strong view of what was right and what was wrong and what our values were as a family, and I think that helped us to get through lots of stuff-including his subsequent departure-very quickly and relatively unscathed because we already had as a threesome that close-knit security and knowledge that this is the way our life is. Indeed our life carried on as normal, pretty much, with minimal disruption.

Sometimes, as your children go through all the landmarks of growing up, you feel your single parenthood very keenly and it can seem a lonely road. When my eldest had his first day at school I had one of those moments. He looked so adorable, all dressed up in his smart new uniform and clutching his schoolbag and his brand new lunch box. It broke my heart not to be able to share that moment of parental pride with his Dad (who was living his new life away from us and away on holiday at the time). Naturally, as the main carer (and since their father lives a considerable distance away) I have taken the lion's share of responsibility for their education and extra-curricular activities.

My boys belonged to a youth group and I found myself volunteering as a leader. This involved such character-building activities as trudging uphill through the pouring rain in the dark with a wailing child to reach a freezing youth hostel. My personal favourite was a three hour hike through fields in the height of summer and hay fever season, eyes and nose streaming all the way! This was followed by spending the night in a remote campsite trying to quiet giggling children (their mood exuberant after playing war games in the woods, singing songs and toasting unappetising wet dough on a stick over the campfire) and the prospect of a visit to the "dunny"—which one of us lucky adults would have to set up and dismantle later-cooking a full English fry up the next morning and washing up in greasy cold water before dismantling all the tents! I remember another occasion where we had to safely shepherd our group of children on a crumbling path next to a river in full flood. As usual, it was a walk of several hours (not helped by my blisters), most of it along the edge of a cliff, and one of the children in my group kept sitting down and refusing to go any further! Then there were the craft evenings, where twenty or so over-excited children would be let loose with a range of messy and potentially dangerous materials ranging from candle wax and paint to scissors, card, glue and papier mache. Our job would be to assist the little darlings to create their masterpieces as quickly and happily as possible so they'd have something to take home and then try and remove the evidence in even less time so that we'd be allowed to use the rented hall again! I have to admit, though, that whilst many of these experiences most definitely took me out of my comfort zone, there were some magical moments which I wouldn't have missed for the world. One of these was the beautiful Burning the Clocks procession (dating back from pagan times), where each child made a lantern using willow twigs and papier mache and our group joined a teeming throng of people wending their way through the streets of the city of Brighton at night, glowing lanterns held aloft, before the stunning finale on the beach, which included music and fireworks and the bonfire to end all bonfires. I got to sleep in a hammock, which was surprisingly comfortable, and helping our adopted child in Haiti and finding out about Fairtrade and the co-operative movement was very heart-warming and educational. I also know how much my sons and I benefitted from our involvement with this group. There were some extremely dedicated leaders who made great role models for the children and a wonderful mixture of personalities and backgrounds, girls and boys, both able-bodied and disabled.

Even the inconvenient things, or things that you might regard as a chore at the outset, can be turned into happy events. As a single parent struggling with the day to day aspects of life as the only adult in the household, it would be tempting to opt out of extra work or involvement in the fund raising or community projects and social, sporting or school-orientated events that you are invited to. Let's face it, you would have a perfectly good excuse to say that you had too much on your plate already. Yet the fact remains that you'll probably gain just as much if not more from interacting and getting involved, as the group or event or activity will from having you on board. There's nothing as good for snapping you out of unhappiness or dissatisfaction with your lot as helping other people. You'll make some good friends and allies along the way and your kids will benefit from the interaction with others, too.

Helen *Stuff like school plays and so on didn't really bother me. I'd always done it on my own so it didn't make any difference. Even if we'd still been together, he wouldn't have gone along anyway. In the early days a weekend would be hard because we didn't have that conventional family unit. That's why I would have friends over. I didn't want to bother my married friends at the weekend because they were all doing family things. It was the single ones who came over.*

Kayleigh *I was really lucky with the Elementary school my son went to, to have teachers who were very understanding of my situation. Maybe they were in the same situation or they knew of others who were single parents also, but they would sometimes mention at a parent teacher conference that they were aware of other parents in the same situation, whether it was single parents or a parent that was ill—whatever it was, I think they were very sympathetic. I just lucked out that way.*

Elaine *When they were at school we were possibly one of the first families to be splitting up, so when it came to doing things like making Christmas cards to take home it was very difficult. But sadly by the time they'd left school it was almost the norm that Mummy and Daddy weren't together. I think that now it's so common for this to happen that the schools are more set up to deal sensitively with those kinds of situations.*

I have pretty much attended every single parent teacher evening, sports day, school open day and school play—sometimes accompanied by my mum but generally by myself, although my husband's parents (who are extremely devoted grandparents) have always tried to attend the important occasions, like concerts, sports days and school plays. This is sometimes awkward, depending on the progress of the divorce—or the often tricky aftermath-but I have always appreciated their efforts and their dedication. It seems well worth a bit of discomfort on my part for the kids to know that they are loved and supported by their proud family, on both sides. They are far too old to be doing one now, but when it came to the annual school nativity play in their primary school I used to take a wad of tissues in my bag, as it always brought our family situation home to me in a very poignant way. Christmas and other holidays can sometimes present a problem, too—even now. Not only do our kids have two homes, but they also have two Christmases and two birthdays and in some ways for children this can be quite a bonus! So there are always different ways of looking at it.

However, there are events, occasions and rituals that have a special significance or sentimental attachment for everyone and I have found at times like these that memories and emotions can still knock me sideways. Even when you think that you're all sorted and reconciled to the way your new life is these days, don't beat yourself up or feel embarrassed if you occasionally find it's all too much to cope with. You're only human after all and you've been so brave and worked so hard to get to where you are now.

CHAPTER EIGHT

TIME FOR YOU

Creating a Sanctuary
Recharging Your Batteries
Making the Most of Time
When Your Ex Has the Kids

Emer *As a single parent the most important thing that you can do, I think, is to keep your individuality and your independence. As well as being a mother and providing everything you can for your child, you also have to keep yourself in check because if you're not happy or you're depressed and isolated and you don't have the support then I can imagine it would be an awful lot more difficult.*

"Only one thing has to change for us to know happiness in our lives: where we focus our attention."

— Greg Anderson

I made the decision right from the start that I would not use my children as pawns in my battles with their Dad and that they should always go visit him together, although I could perhaps have argued that the baby was too young to be parted from me. However, as they grew older I was glad of my decision because I know to this day that they are always looking out for each other on their weekends with their father and if one of them is homesick or having a hard time with something, his brother is there to reassure and support him. If your child does not have siblings, be assured that it is vital for children to know and spend time with both parents if at all possible.

At the same time, some of you do not have this option. My friend's ex totally disappeared, leaving a trail of unpaid child support behind him. As the sole breadwinner and carer it has been a struggle for her to balance a busy full-time job with other demands, let alone time for herself, but luckily she has a very supportive family and her son gets to spend weekends and some of the holidays with his grandparents, aunt and uncle and cousins. His female cousins have cuddled him and played with him and thanks to his male cousin and his uncle he has been able to hone his football, table tennis and cricket skills and been taken sailing. His grandparents have been strict but loving. His grandmother has read stories to him and cooked him her finest food and thanks to his Grandpa, he is now good at backgammon, Scrabble and Othello!

If, unlike my friend, you do not have a large and supportive family there is other help available. Perhaps your child can spend time with a trusted friend, neighbour or family that you know? Your friend's teenager might be delighted to get some babysitting practice and give you a welcome break by taking your child to the park or playing with them. In every community you will find support groups and babysitting circles to join. If you are unsure, ask your doctor or health worker about what help is available for single mums in your area.

At first, when I had to give my children to my ex for his access weekends I felt completely bereft. I remember that I would repeatedly pack and repack their bag before they left, feeling incredibly anxious that I would forget their favourite toys or that they wouldn't have enough clothes to keep them warm and dry. Of course, what I was really worrying about was that I wasn't there to protect them and look after them. In a well-meaning gesture, my ex and his parents compiled a video with some footage of the boys on his weekends and gave it to me "from the boys". All I can remember is the shot of my youngest, still only a small baby, sitting by himself and crying whilst his brother and the grown-ups ignored him. I'm sure that shortly afterwards somebody picked him up and comforted him but it upset me dreadfully, and to this day I have never watched the video again.

When the children had been collected I used to wander through the eerily quiet and empty house and into their bedrooms, usually in floods of tears. But then a wise friend, herself a veteran single mum, gave me some advice. First of all she explained to me that whilst I was visualising my ex and the other woman playing happy families with my kids in a "shiny, happy people" kind of way, the reality might be very different. There's no more effective passion-killer than a broken night's sleep, a small wriggly person jumping on your bed at 6 am or a day of potty training. Added to this, my ex's girlfriend (who had no children of her own) would undoubtedly be trying to prove that she was not only willing to look after his children but also enthusiastic and capable. It can be hard playing the Miss Congeniality role with children who are extra-cranky and difficult due to adjusting to having a new woman in their life–a fact I later discovered with my own stepchildren!

Once my friend had reassured me with a reality check, she then went on to underline the importance of doing something fun *and* something constructive on my child-free weekends. I followed her advice to the letter and still do today now that my boys are 13 and 16. There's always a job that needs doing which would easier to complete with no distractions. This could range from mowing the lawn or cutting the hedge to redecorating a room in your house. It might even be catching up with the ironing or doing a big shop and cooking a huge batch of Bolognese, casserole or soup before dividing it up into portions, bagging them and freezing them ready for grabbing and reheating on a busy school night when you still want to give your kids something wholesome and home-made. But all work and no play makes Jill a very dull girl. And I know that to begin with, you may feel too tired or miserable to do anything other than crawl under the duvet or slouch on the sofa with only an old film and a box of tissues for company. Now, I'm not knocking the idea of a duvet day or watching TV for hours on end. Indeed, one of the joys of being single is that you get to choose exactly how you spend your alone time. If you want to stay up all night eating ice cream from the tub and reading your book, or lie in bed till midday just because you can, then GO FOR IT! But don't fall into the trap of moping all weekend just because you're single now and feeling sad. I made it a rule to always organise at least one nice outing per childless weekend and I still do to this day. This could mean going to a party, out with friends, or having someone over for coffee, lunch or supper. It could mean going to see that new film, trying out a new bar or having a drink at your local pub, having a massage, walking round an exhibition, sight-seeing -anything you like as long as you are going to have company and have some fun. Even if it feels like an effort, do it and I promise you that nine times out of ten it will give you a much-needed boost to your morale. You deserve it.

Rachel I think having a few treats to look forward to is important. Try and do something every day which you enjoy. This may be phoning a friend or a member of the family or spending time with them, playing with your child/children, reading a book, playing some music, going for a walk or swim or doing some yoga or exercise of some kind, doing something creative like painting a picture, going to a gallery, baking a cake or relaxing by having a really nice long soak in the bath, or just having some 'me' time.

Kayleigh And of course I did have some free time when my son went to his dad's every other weekend, so I got a little bit of time to myself. That's something that I feel is very important as a parent or a single parent. Make sure you do have that time away or that time alone, even if it's an hour or a half hour or a day. Whatever it is, take a break, because it's a lot of work – 24/7! I tried to get out and go to a movie, see friends or do that kind of thing. There were things that I did have to catch up on, too, so having a whole weekend was really nice; I could have one day for me and then one day for the laundry, the grocery shopping, the cleaning and all of that. So that was a good balance and that's probably what kept me sane! Whatever situation you're in, I think you have to realise the benefits and the good points and avoid "the grass is always greener" syndrome!

Emer *I had a supportive family. They didn't live near me but they were always there. I had great friends, my daughter was great and you just kind of made the best out of whatever situation that you had. I think also the balance is important of me having my time with my friends and with my family—both with my daughter and without her as well. I had a couple of very good friends around me here in Brighton so if, for instance there was something on, my good friend (who actually moved over here and lives down the road at the moment) would just step in and say: "You need a night out. Let's go". Also, even if it's not ideal to not be with the father of your child, if you still have a good relationship you do get a couple of times a week to be able to go out and see friends, and that's been really good. Even at this point, with my daughter still going round to her dad's we actually have a choice twice a week whether to go out or not. And although we're not going out as much now as we did in the old days, that choice, that ability to go away for weekends is great.*

Helen *When you talk about what to do with your time when the kids are away with their Dad, my immediate thought is "What a luxury!" because I didn't have that, and I'm sure a lot of other women don't. The only me time is when they go to bed. I only had 2 years on my own and I did get a babysitter but I didn't go out much because of money. There really was no time for me but that was fine-it was my choice to have them, after all.*

"What is free time? I'm a single mother. My free moments are filled with loving my little girl."

—Roma Downey

So how about when you don't have a whole weekend but just need to recharge your batteries? In my case I looked forward to my long soak in a hot bath in the evening once the boys were in bed. I usually took a book and a drink but you might choose just some scented bath oil and a candle. Use your creativity to change the energy from the hectic day with kids to a relaxed evening vibe.

Many mothers have spoken to me about how important it was to them to decorate or renovate their homes, making them into somewhere safe and welcoming for themselves and their children–a new start for their new life, if you like.

Elaine When I moved into this house it was an absolute tip, so nearly every evening, after the kids had gone to bed, I'd be decorating.

Even if you don't have the energy or the funds to redecorate your entire home, it can be wonderful to create a soothing sanctuary inside your home for yourself where you can feel more peaceful and recharge your batteries. If you have a spare room this can be set aside, but for many single mothers the only available option is their bedroom. Have fun designing your sanctuary. Choose colours you like and softer lighting. Try to keep it clutter and toy free as you want to minimise distractions to your relaxation. You might like to hang artwork which you find inspiring or restful to look at. Many people swear by the Feng Shui, the Chinese art of placement, for creating a harmonious environment and encouraging a positive flow of energy (in this room or indeed the rest of the house). There are many good books on the subject. For an introduction you might find **The Complete Idiot's Guide to Feng Shui, 3rd Edition (Complete Idiot's Guides (Lifestyle Paperback) by Master Val Biktashev** a good place to start. You might still find it hard to relax, even when your bedroom is more conducive to relaxation. I recommend a positive, affirming Hypnosis CD to refresh, relax and comfort you–good to play when the house is finally quiet. A lot of people have the wrong idea about hypnosis. You actually have total control the whole time–it's just like slipping into a pleasant daydream and should one of the children need you, you can awaken instantly and feel alert and awake. You can find a range of empowering Hypnosis CDs on my website:.**www. thelifeyoudeserve.co.uk**.

CHAPTER NINE

WORKING AS A
SINGLE MOTHER

Finding Child Care

Learning New Skills To
Help You Manage the House

The Power of the Mums' Network

Asking For Help

"In truth, I am a single mother. But I don't feel alone at all in parenting my daughter. Krishna has a whole other side of her family who loves her, too. And so Krishna is parented by me, but also by her grandmother and aunts and cousins and uncles and friends."

—Padma Lakshmi

Helen I had no back-up. Although I had a sister near here, she didn't do anything. I had a cousin down the road and I thought she would have helped me, too, but I got nothing. It was very hard and I didn't have any family help, but having said that, I had a friend who helped me move in and two of my other friends were very good, so I wasn't totally on my own. You survive because you have to. You do it for your children. Luckily, the road I picked to live in was all front doors open, same aged children, so that was brilliant. I relocated and although I could have ended up in one area which would have been a disaster, I was very lucky with the location I picked, for sure. Check out the area, especially the school. They could have gone to one school which was notorious; it had a real reputation for being a rough school. I was thinking of the kids growing up and the people I wanted them to mix with. So I think the school was a really big part of it.

Rachel Another issue is not being able to delegate tasks to the father. Single mums also have to do all the admin and paperwork for their household, as well as the majority of the cleaning, even if children are encouraged to help with household chores.

I've always found housework and staying tidy to be an effort, something that doesn't come easily to me. I'm one of those people with a tidy mind but a tendency to have an untidy environment. When I was a single mum it just seemed overwhelming, especially with a tiny baby and a three year old. Even today, with older children and a supportive husband, I get stressed and overwhelmed and behind on housework and laundry sometimes. There's a wonderful free website that you can join (which a friend recommended to me), called **http://www. flylady.net**. What I like about their system is the lack of judgment. They also recognise that creative, spontaneous personalities like me (or Side-tracked Home Executives, as Flylady, Marla Cilley, calls them) are fed up with living in CHAOS (Can't Have Anyone Over Syndrome)! If you were not "born organised", then this is the system for you. Using a quick and easy series of routines, the Flylady way will get rid of your procrastination, your clutter and your dirt in just a few minutes a day. After a while, the routines become second nature and you gradually work your way round the whole house without having to do massive spring-cleans, because you are cleaning more efficiently as you get rid of clutter. You get sent emails on a regular basis to keep you on track which are motivational and supportive without being nagging (her strapline is "You are not behind! I don't want you to try to catch up; I just want you to jump in where we are. O.K.?") and there's even a daily Flykids Challenge, to help you teach the children some good habits.

Kayleigh *Having a support system, especially when you're raising children on your own is really important because sometimes there are going to be those moments when you feel alone —you know, you come home every day and you have to deal with all this stuff by yourself. The father might be nearby but inevitably you come home to the house and here are your kids, and you're working and having to take care of all the day-to-day stuff which is very time-consuming. So my friends were really good. I'd moved 70 miles away from my family but I met new people through work. I do remember so many times connecting with other moms who had kids the same age and taking them to the pumpkin patch at Halloween or taking them Trick or Treating or to the park. That was a nice outing for me to talk to the moms, have the adult company and also spend time with the kids, so that was really huge and helped keep me grounded. I fed off the other moms and got advice, and they're telling stories and you're thinking: "Oh my Gosh, I can relate to that! I'm not alone and everybody's going through this in different ways—it's difficult being a parent but it's so rewarding at the same time."*

Elaine *All the kids were a similar age and they all played together and that just made everything so much easier. We never felt alone because we had almost an extended family around us. I also kept most of our joint friends that I'd had when I was married and they looked after me.*

Emer *I took a year out between my degree and my Honours degree and had a year off with my daughter. That first year we went travelling to Sweden for three weeks, which was great. She's extremely easy to travel with so I never let having her hold me back. I think at that stage, when I was 21, I'd already caught the travel bug and I used to spend all my summers travelling around Europe or other countries. The first year that I was just by myself with her was amazing and I think one of my favourite years ever. I think I really learned to be extremely independent, take back control of my life-my financial life, my home life. I focused a lot on us. We went on little adventures, we travelled back home.*

I had no family down in Galway but I had great friends, so even when my boyfriend moved out and we broke up, I always had a friend living with me. That made the difference in terms of just little things like taking showers or popping out to the shops, and things like that.

"I've learned that every working mom is a superwoman."

—Uma Thurman

Rachel *Anyone who has read **"I Don't Know How She Does It" by Alison Pearson** (published by Vintage UK, Random House) based on a true life story and now made into a film, will sympathise where the diarist in the book tells about the agony of children's birthday parties where she spent time "distressing" mince pies (which she had actually bought from Marks and Spencer) so she could pass them off as her own home-baked version, because she felt guilty and inadequate as a mum because she worked full-time. In the book she was the only working mother and baked her child's birthday cake–albeit at 3 in the morning–to show she could do that too, as well as being a successful businesswoman in the city!*

Emer *My boyfriend and I were supposed to move to Canada or New Zealand but that didn't work out. I was in a desperate place for a little while but then I used that as a spur to come over here and finish my studies. So we moved over here to England to do my postgraduate studies up in London. So it was almost like a blessing in disguise. Although it was incredibly difficult to go through, she did kind of help me. When I was in second year Art College, I was a very typical student who was going out too much and drinking too much and not focused and almost failing Art College (which is really hard to do!). But I went from almost failing to being awarded Student of the Year and getting Distinctions for both my degrees, so she gave me that focus.*

My post grad was only meant to be a year but ended up being three years' study. Now I'm back in Uni again, doing my teacher training, so I'm the eternal student!

I'm teaching at a college at the moment. I was a Visual Arts Developer in a high school for two years and then I went for this teaching job. I was given the job without having any teacher qualification. Because it's a college you're able to do that—it's not like a primary school. So I was given the job on the understanding that I would take up my teacher training at some stage. So I started straight away. It's taken two years part time but it's been a great way to do it because I've been working the whole way through. The one year's intense PGCE course is quite difficult but has allowed me to spread it out a bit more.

"I was raised by a single mother who made a way for me. She used to scrub floors as a domestic worker, put a cleaning rag in her pocketbook and ride the subways in Brooklyn so I would have food on the table. But she taught me as I walked her to the subway that life is about not where you start, but where you're going. That's family values."

—Al Sharpton

"My mom was a source of strength. She showed me by example that women, regardless of how difficult life may get, can do it all."

—Gloria Estefan

Rachel *I took opportunities to improve our situation in the way I could through my work, which included going back to full time work, getting a promotion and applying and getting a job involving going abroad to a third world country. This proved to be one of the best things we did, even if it meant going to court to enable us to do so. I had an interesting and stimulating job and I was able to offer my son a better standard of living. My son, who already had knowledge of different cultures and religions, due to his time at a diverse and multi-cultural school in London, enjoyed his time there and he made friends of many nationalities. It also showed him there are lots more unfortunate children than he and it opened his perspective. Whilst we were there we kept in close touch with friends and family, including having regular visits to the UK and having visitors to stay. This helped greatly with settling back home again. I was also able to find a place for him in the same school when we returned to the UK, which really helped.*

Kayleigh But as for finding day care and after school programmes, for those of us who were single-or just working parents-that was really hard. There was a network that would help you find day care, and after doing some research and talking to friends I discovered a child-minder who lived just a few houses down from me, which was really incredible. But when you find this really great person that you trust with your child's life and they tell you "we're going to be moving", then it's stressful, because that did happen. I think there's more out there now for the daytime help. The thing I see is lacking the most now, though, is for people who maybe work odd hours. In this economic climate, those might be the only hours that someone can find work. If you're not with a big company that provides a crèche you are literally juggling all the time.

Elaine I was lucky to have met some wonderful friends who helped look after the kids, but at one stage I had to find a child minder. The firm I worked for at the time had a scheme where they put you in touch with a local child minder, and I was so lucky to find one that had a space. She and her husband were the sort of people who would, knowing that you were on your own, introduce you to everybody else.

Rachel One of my biggest challenges has been holding down a busy full-time job whilst being the sole carer and provider. Sorting out wraparound care was important in my situation. The cost of childcare in all this is a key challenge.

There are some schools which are aimed at offering flexible hours to cover the working day for parents. Some schools have breakfast clubs and after school clubs. But these can sometimes be expensive. Sometimes the informal network can work really well. I found someone who lived round the corner who offered a breakfast club from the crack of dawn and walked the children to school. I found working really helpful when I was going through a bad time. It meant I could focus on something else, use my grey cells, use other skills, be professional, look smart and interact with others, and very few people would know what I was going through. There is evidence that being busy really helps people with getting on and out of a difficult situation.

Being in a job which allows some flexibility is also important. I asked if I would be able to request to work from home 2 days a week to enable me to reduce the travelling time and cut down on childcare costs. This made a huge difference to me and made me feel more in control and less stretched generally. It is best to be clear with your employer about what work-related commitments are realistically possible and explain why you may need some understanding of your situation and why you may *need flexibility. Even the PM and Deputy PM arrange important regular Cabinet meetings at a time which enables them to be able to take their children to school. Equally, if you are the sole carer, then it is even more important that you go to the parent-teacher meetings or the Christmas play. Flexibility works both ways and there are usually ways of making up the time.*

Juggling children, divorce and financial matters by yourself can be an eye-opener and result in varying amounts of chaos. Here is an extract from my diary at the time, which I entitled *"Just an ordinary day"*.

6.45 a.m. I am awoken from a deep sleep to hear Pepper the spaniel barking furiously in the kitchen. Bleary-eyed, I go down and let her out into the garden.

7.25 a.m. My solicitor rings (I like a man who's dedicated to his job!) to say that my mortgage offer has arrived and therefore I will need to drop in to his office sometime this morning and sign the paperwork.

8 a.m. My four year old is sitting in the baby's cot on a pile of clean, previously-ironed clothes that he needed for their game and has therefore taken out of the cupboard. The cot is a boat, he explains. He is the captain and his brother is the baby captain. He scowls fiercely when I ask him to get out, clutches his brother to him in a gesture of defiance and refuses to budge. Eventually I cajole him out of the cot so I can pick the baby up and change his nappy.

8.50 a.m. We're on the road at last. I've piled the dog, boys, spare nappies and baby wipes into the car, along with bank statements, property details and divorce papers. We should just make it to playschool on time. My eldest is drinking apple juice from a beaker and finishing his bread and jam soldiers. When we stop at the traffic lights I give the baby a quick gulp from his bottle. Suddenly we meet a huge queue of traffic. There has been an accident and several essential parts of my route are now closed. As I navigate my way via the back roads to nursery school, my little boy pipes up from the back seat:

"What's an accident?"

"Whose fault was it?"

"What were they doing?"

"How fast were they going?"

He is still a little deaf from his cold, so all my replies must be given in a loud voice, despite my sore throat!

9.25a.m. Reach nursery school and deposit my son. Drive 20 minutes to the solicitor's office. My mum kindly meets me in the car park and entertains the baby, whilst I race in to sign the mortgage documents. Load packing cases from my Mum's car into mine (ready to start packing up in preparation for the move), then make a quick stop to buy more nappies. I cannot exchange contracts until my house insurance is in place. Receive call on mobile from insurance brokers, to say that all their computers are down, so no quotations will be possible for the time being!

10.45a.m. Arrive at my sister's house. Take dog for walk around her field, then frantically fill in my tax return (she's an accountant, so she can help me) and calculate the amount of tax I'll have to pay. Meanwhile, my school friend rings to discuss my son's page boy outfit for her forthcoming wedding.

12.00 Must pack up and get the baby into the car to collect his brother from nursery.

12.45p.m. Arrive home. Prepare lunch. Ring brokers regarding the insurance. Parcel up ill-fitting velvet page boy trousers. Write covering letter to tax office.

2.00p.m. Take kids across road to local post office to photocopy tax return before sending it off. No photocopier. Walk 5 minutes to another shop. No photocopier there, either. Buy my eldest a lolly. Walk home again. Post parcel.

3.00p.m. Solicitor rings to announce that exchange of contracts has happened on my new house. Hooray! Drive to Horsham, the nearest big town. Collect parcel containing my son's page boy shoes from sorting office. Drive to Office World to photocopy tax return. Tax return not in my handbag. Help! Frantic search of car. Drive home. Children are by now fast asleep in their car seats. Leave them strapped safely into their seats, lock car and run into house. Tax return not here either. Ring postal sorting office to see if they have found envelope containing tax return. No luck. Say anguished prayer. My sister has spent hours doing my accounts and helping me to complete this form. She may never speak to me again if we have to redo the whole thing! Just as I am rushing out of the house again I hear the car alarm. One of the children must have woken up and set it off. Both of them are crying. Must get a bottle of milk for the baby and calm them both down. Explain that we must go back to Horsham to search post office pavement for missing envelope. This news does not go down well with my son! Bribe him with promise of treat if he is good.

4.15p.m. Drive to Horsham. Hallelujah! Envelope discovered outside post office! Load children into Office World trolley and wheel them in to get form photocopied. Shop assistant comments on how cute they are. They are! I love them, I love them!

Next stop: supermarket to buy food and petrol. Have to stop at entrance so my son can have a ride on Sesame Street car at entrance. Half way round supermarket: "Mummy, I need a wee!" Run round remaining aisles, throwing items in at random as I pass. Girl at checkout agrees to start packing groceries into bags for me whilst I run with boys to toilets in far corner of shopping complex. Just get back in time to avoid being lynched by impatient man in queue behind me.

9.00p.m. Children are bathed and in bed. Just preparing my "Exchange-of-Contracts- Celebration-Meal for One" and looking forward to some peace and quiet and a chance to put my feet up, when I hear the ominous patter of small feet descending the stairs. My son can't sleep because there are monsters in his room. Also he needs cereal, needs another drink of milk. Eat my meal with a small, hyperactive child clambering on the sofa cushions above my head. Narrowly avoid wearing my meal.

10.00 The end of another hectic day! The house looks like a medium-sized hurricane has passed through it. There is a large, overflowing laundry basket full of ironing sitting reproachfully in the corner of the room. The main thing is, though, that I'm still here, I'm still sane (just!), my precious babies are safely tucked up in their beds and sleeping soundly and I'm well on the way (after months in temporary accommodation) to putting down some permanent roots. Life is looking up!

Kayleigh *I was just so busy with being a mom and there were a lot of things that I struggled with, whether it was finances or time or my son. For me personally it's always been difficult to reach out for help when I feel like I need it, rather than wait until I'm absolutely desperate. I think it's really nice as a parent to have help, whether it's a support group or talking to a friend, whatever's needed-just a sounding board for you. Because when you're a single mom you go home and you don't have anybody to vent about your day to. When you get home you're just there by yourself dealing with everything. So I would have found that really helpful. When I was able to talk things through, get it out of my system and not let it boil inside it was a release, and it calmed me down and helped me carry on and deal with what I needed to deal with. So reach out and communicate with someone before it becomes an emergency. When you have that negative energy and stress, when you're under duress you don't make the decisions or deal with things in the way that you should. So, waiting until that point when you can feel that things are starting to get stressful, feeling your body tense up, knowing that you need to let it out, that's the time to act. Whether it's talking* *to someone or going for a walk or a run, or getting some exercise, take some time to recognise that and do what you need to do to get back on track, in order to be the best mom you can be and be happy, too, with yourself. Don't feel guilty about that because it's not selfish to look after yourself so that you can take care of others effectively.*

CHAPTER TEN

THE FORGIVENESS PROCESS

Boy, this is a big one...so big for me, in fact, that I nearly didn't write this chapter at all and I can honestly say that thinking about what I was going to write brought up all sorts of emotional baggage for me. This, of course is why I had to knuckle down and deal with what came up for me, so that I could give you some insight into the process and help in achieving forgiveness-not only of others, but also of yourself. I have also deliberately not put this chapter in at the start of the book as I personally feel that everyone needs a little time and perspective when dealing with this issue, and in the very early days it's just too much to ask.

"Always forgive your enemies-nothing annoys them so much."

—Oscar Wilde

"There is no revenge so complete as forgiveness."

—Josh Billings

"How does one know if she has forgiven? You tend to feel sorrow over the circumstance instead of rage, you tend to feel sorry for the person rather than angry with him. You tend to have nothing left to say about it all."

—Clarissa Pinkola Estes

"To understand is to forgive, even oneself."

—Alexander Chase

"I don't know if I continue, even today, always liking myself. But what I learned to do many years ago was to forgive myself. It is very important for every human being to forgive herself or himself because if you live, you will make mistakes-it is inevitable. But once you do and you see the mistake, then you forgive yourself and say, "Well, if I'd known better I'd have done better," that's all. So you say to people who you think you may have injured, "I'm sorry," and then you say to yourself, "I'm sorry." If we all hold on to the mistake, we can't see our own glory in the mirror because we have the mistake between our faces and the mirror; we can't see what we're capable of being. You can ask forgiveness of others, but in the end the real forgiveness is in one's own self."

—Maya Angelou

"As we know, forgiveness of oneself is the hardest of all the forgivenesses."

—Joan Baez

"When there's that forgiveness present and compassion, it just helps you live so much easier".

—Craig T. Nelson

I distinctly remember asking my counsellor at the beginning if I could still move on with my life without forgiving my ex. It seemed to me that his betrayal and infidelity were just too awful to forgive. How could I forgive behaviour that I felt to my core was immoral and wrong? Didn't forgiving him mean that I condoned what he had done?

"Forgiveness isn't about condoning what has happened to you or someone else's actions against you."

—Jennifer O'Neill

Was it possible to accept what had happened and forgive, whilst still being very clear that I would never agree that what had happened was justifiable? Would it mean that they (he and "the other woman") had won? It seemed like a battle, as break-ups and divorces inevitably do, with all the arguing about money, access to the children, behaviour and blame. Because I'd already lost so much, I didn't want to give them the satisfaction of yet another victory over me. So, in effect, not only would they have won but I would have the indignity of losing face if I ever climbed down from the moral high ground which I clung to like a life raft for so many years.

"Forgiveness means letting go of the past."

—Gerald Jampolsky

Would it at some point be possible, I wondered, for me to forgive him privately in my own mind without going "on record" about it? If I couldn't bring myself to totally forgive him, could I at least release the bitterness and achieve an indifference or acceptance of what had happened?

"When you forgive, you in no way change the past-but you sure do change the future."

—Bernard Meltzer

Elaine I avoid contact where possible because I'm still very bitter. I think it's because he's never admitted that he was to blame. I know it's not his fault exactly, because alcoholism is a disease, but he never takes any responsibility and he has never given any money towards the children, and doesn't want to. That's something I find very hard to swallow, because even in sober moments, surely he would realise he had a duty to provide for them? I don't think I've ever really forgiven him, but I've moved on regardless. The fact that that I haven't forgiven him at this stage is neither here nor there because I never bump into him, so it's a little bit like "out of sight, out of mind".

Angela So for me it was affirmations. I got really into affirmations. They saved my life! I love Louise Hay. I've read a lot, done so much forgiveness work. I remember pulling out cards that said "reach deep inside and draw on your inner strength" and saying "I don't want to do that any more!" but then the feisty part of me came out, and my friends would invite me out dancing, and I just said to myself: "I'm not going to let him rob one more day of joy from my life! This is not going to happen. He hasn't got the power to do this." And now I really just try and apply that philosophy. I completely embrace the concept of forgiveness.

There's a Louise Hay exercise, "The person I need to forgive is ….I forgive them for……" (and you name it) and then you say: "Thank you, I set you free". And then you repeat it. It took me days to do this. And then you feel lightness, a lifting off. Joseph Murphy also has some amazing writing around forgiving people. I also insatiably do journaling; I do angel cards, all kinds of stuff. So my life is fantastic. And he says to me "Now you can do everything that you could never do when you were with me", and it's true, whereas he's back in that misery.

> "To forgive is to sincerely wish for the other what you wish for yourself."
>
> —Joseph Murphy

There was a time not so long ago when I started to have terrible dreams about all the people in my life who have hurt me or let me down. The plots changed and became a changing cast of characters over successive nights. These ranged from my first and second husbands, childhood and college friends, a scary ex-employer and a dear friend from schooldays who now has a new life and interests and no longer makes time for our friendship. The one thing they had in common was that they were all people who had left me with unresolved feelings of sadness, hurt, loss and resentment. It may well have been that writing this book and going over painful old ground had dredged up all these old wounds and brought them up for me to look at and resolve once and for all. You may well find that at a time of great stress and emotion in your life, such as the events that caused you to find yourself starting out again as a single mother, you have a similar experience of introspection. This can be a very uncomfortable process, but one thing I have learned in my own work as a transformational coach, hypnotist and Beyond NLP practitioner (not to mention in my own life) is that emotions will continue to resurface until you deal with them, so this can be a liberating and cleansing time for you if you only let it. Forgiveness of yourself and others and the process of letting go of these emotions and thoughts that no longer serve you can finally free you from the shackles that would otherwise hold you back and impede the fantastic progress that you are making with your new life.

> "To forgive is to set a prisoner free and discover that the prisoner was you."
>
> —Lewis B. Smedes

As my wise and valued friend and colleague Dawn Tarter wrote to me at the time of my own personal "forgiveness crisis":

"You are doing a remarkable thing for yourself, a very transformative and important thing for yourself as you release relationships that no longer serve you. Celebrate this time-this is growth. You can release those old relationships with light and love and bon voyage or you can tell them to bugger off. Whichever is right for you and that relationship. You are transforming and releasing. Becoming a butterfly."

I am happy to report that I had a wonderful insight after working through these issues myself and that was: if I acted as a useful springboard for all these people from the past as they moved on to other phases of their lives without me, then it just goes to prove that the coaching I am qualified to do is my perfect job. Now I get to help people and heal them, but they pay me for my efforts and I don't get left feeling hurt and resentful when they choose to move on.

"Forgiveness is a gift you give yourself."

—Suzanne Somers

"Forgiveness is not always easy. At times, it feels more painful than the wound we suffered, to forgive the one that inflicted it. And yet, there is no peace without forgiveness."

—Marianne Williamson

Moving Towards Completion
by Francine Kaye

So what can you do on a practical level to start moving forward with your life? Take some time to answer the following questions. They will help you to see the cobwebs of your relationship clinging to the corners of your mind, and get some way towards completing the process of letting go.

1. *I am still angry at you for....*
2. *I am angry at myself for .....*
3. *I am sad because I think I should have .....*
4. *And I think you should have ......*
5. *Sometimes you reminded me of .....*
6. *And I reacted by.....*
7. *I wish we could have.....*
8. *I am sorry for.....*
9. *I want to acknowledge you for .....*
10. *I want to acknowledge me for.....*
11. *I need to forgive myself for sometimes.....*
12. *I need to forgive you for sometimes.....*
13. *Through knowing you I learned.....*
14. *This has given me.....*
15. *I enriched your life by.....*
16. *I wish for you.....*
17. *I wish for myself.....*
18. *You owe me nothing.....*

19. I owe you nothing.....
20. I am complete.

HELP AND HEALING TIPS

There are several wonderful processes that your Beyond NLP practitioner can take you through in order to achieve closure and peace and release old relationships (or the negative residue they leave). One of the most effective of these is the Forgiveness Process. One of the things I like most about it is that you don't ever have to tell your practitioner or anyone who is showing up on your list of significant people, who is being removed, who is staying, or anything at all about the process. It is completely private. And you are in an absolutely safe place emotionally throughout.

For details of your local practitioner, please see the list at the end of the book. Alternatively, send an email to vivienne@thelifeyoudeserve.co.uk and I will forward you the contact details of someone who will be able to help you.

CHAPTER ELEVEN

DATING AGAIN – DOS AND DON'TS

"I don't think it's necessarily healthy to go into relationships as a needy person. Better to go in with a full deck."

—Anjelica Huston

Angela I think sometimes when I look at old photos, how long was he unhappy? How long had he been feeling like that, because he never said? And I can't even ask him that question because he's such a chronic liar that you wouldn't get a true answer from him. According to the kids, his new wife's family have paid for him to go to counselling for years but he just lies to the counsellor. He just says what he thinks people want to hear! I went through quite a long time of thinking that I had totally, erroneously, raised my kids wrong—that I had set them up for failure in the world because I had raised them to be decent and honourable and honest and to trust people, and if this was what the world was **really** like then I was not preparing them for the real world. Friends would hear about something that my ex had done and they'd say "But people just **can't do** that!" And I'd say "Yes, people can do **whatever they want.**" You might have this conception that people can't treat each other like that but actually, they can! My eldest daughter is a songwriter too and one of her lines is "So now I hold my cards closer to my chest (I always thought people said what they mean)." How do you believe anybody? If you've been living with someone all those years and you think they're happy but they're not? How do you know what's real any more? It's tough to trust again, right?

Louise At my age now, anyone I got together with would be bound to have some kind of 'baggage' of their own.

Kayleigh Right before I moved out here, my company opened up a new branch and a couple of my friends that I worked with moved out here. My son was about 2 and a half and of course I really wanted to have my own house. I was single and the cost of living in the San Francisco Bay area was very expensive, so that's when I decided to come out here. The cost of living was much lower. I thought: I'll have an opportunity to buy a house. But right before I moved out here I met somebody through work and we started dating. We had been dating for about 6 months before I moved out here, and we carried on dating for about four years after that. He had two children of his own and he was very good with my son. The kids got along really well and he was such a help to me when I moved house, but inevitably the distance made it very difficult and it just kind of fell apart. It got to the point where one of us had to make the decision—either I was going to be moving back, or he was going to be moving out here. It was so hard. He was just the best man that I've ever met (besides *my Dad!) but unfortunately it just didn't work out. After that, as far as dating went I was very careful not to bring people around that I didn't know weren't going to be here for a long time. That was difficult, obviously; there was a lot of talking on the phone because I couldn't see this person all the time—even if there was a connection I was just really hesitant to do that, but I think in the long run it was a good decision. You do have to make those sacrifices sometimes.*

__Elaine__ I do think about retirement. In my line of business, a lot of our clients are quite elderly and it's amazing how many couples there are who are well into their eighties. Some of them are so sweet together and I think "Ahh, maybe that would be nice".

__Annabel__ In terms of being a single parent I was effectively on my own for three or four years. But I had about 18 months after the split before I first made contact with my current partner, before he first popped into my Inbox! I met him online but it took us another 4 months to actually meet. It then took another two years for me to move up to the part of the country where he lived. We were very lucky because he was only the fourth person I'd had contact with this way. I was also incredibly frightened or wary of internet dating, so I did a few emails but I'm not one of these people who could meet up the next night for a drink—no way! He and I are very wordy people so we spent a long time writing and we wrote long missives to each other, and they got more and more frequent. I got to know a lot about his family and his past. There's no way he could have been making it all up because three weeks after I met him I then I met his brother and his sister-in-law, and they are just so much like my family. I knew he was genuine because then I met his parents. His father's from a military background like mine, and you can't make all that up!

__Emer__ For the first eight years of her life it was mainly just me looking after her, and if you don't get a good feeling or if they seem a bit put off by you having this child, I have no time for that whatsoever. I remember one time when I was out and someone came up to chat to me and as soon as I mentioned a child he actually just turned around and walked away. It's the most off-putting thing you could ever come across! And the thing is, the way I saw it—that anyone would be lucky to have my daughter in their lives because she __is__ amazing and everyone is addicted to her.

Elaine I've done the dating websites and several times I've met up with people but I haven't really found it for me. Although three or four people I met up with were very nice men and we had a pleasant hour or two chatting away, I was thinking "What am I doing spending my time with a stranger?" I think the last time I was going to meet up with someone was on a Friday evening and I rang up and said "Look, I'm really sorry to let you down, but I don't think this is for me" because the last thing I wanted to do was to spend a Friday evening after a week at work with a complete stranger. I would rather have gone out with my girlfriends! That's just how I am, I suppose; if it happens it happens and if I really get to the point where I do feel lonely and don't know what to do with myself then I will get up and make a big effort to do something about it. At the moment it's not top on my priority list. A lot of people don't understand that.

The jury's out as to when the best time is to put your toe into the water again and start dating. You'll have to trust your instinct on that one. I remember being very annoyed when someone helpfully told me that it would take at least two years to get over the loss of such a significant relationship. I've always been impatient by nature (impetuous, my family call it) and I didn't want to spend two years under a rock somewhere, waiting to get better! Whilst my sister advised caution, time to lick my wounds, I wanted to find someone to kiss it better. After all, I reasoned: I already felt like my ex had taken all my prettiest years, my youthful years, and here I was starting again at 34, complete with cellulite and stretch marks! I met my first husband very young, and really he was my first serious boyfriend. So all through Art College, when my friends and fellow students were having a wild time dating, there I was in a committed relationship. Each to her own, but I was going to catch up on some of the fun I'd missed out on. There are all sorts of ways of meeting people of course, but I didn't want to hang around hoping to bump into Mr Right at the local supermarket checkout, singles bars didn't appeal to me and a lot of the men I'd come across where I lived seemed to be old age pensioners! I did go on a couple of blind dates organised by well-meaning friends but they were not a success. I realised that whilst your mutual friends might think that you would make the perfect couple, they do not allow for physical chemistry (or lack thereof!)

Then I saw a programme on TV about dating, sponsored by one of the internet dating sites. I thought it might be intriguing to log in and have a look.

It was quite a revelation! I never realised just how many people there were out there–all seemingly like me, too busy to find love but determined not to let a happy future pass them by. I decided to give it a go. I remember that my Mum, in particular, was initially horrified at the idea of me going on to the Internet to find a partner ("Why's a nice girl like you having to resort to doing that?", or something of the sort). I think things were very different when she was young. You could meet a potential partner at the tennis club, or one of the many dances and parties that people seemed to organise. As a self-employed single mum, my options seemed to me to be limited. I didn't go to an office every day, so it was unlikely I'd meet anyone through work unless I started socialising with clients, which didn't seem very professional to me, quite apart from the fact that most of my customers were female.

So began a fascinating, sometimes heart-breaking and often hilarious part of my life.

I discovered that looking through people's profiles was an entertainment in itself. Here is a selection of my favourite profiles–favourite because they made me laugh! (Some details have been changed to protect the identities of these would-be Romeos.)

CRAZY JAMIE

I'm a daring figure, often seen scaling walls and crushing ice. I write award-winning screen plays and manage time efficiently. Occasionally I tread water for three days in a row. I woo ladies with my sensuous tuba playing. I can cook a 30 minute brownie in 20 minutes. I am an expert in the tango, a veteran in love and an outlaw in Peru. Using only a rake and a large bottle of Tequila, I once defended a small village in the Amazon basin from a horde of ferocious army ants. Children adore me. I can hurl tennis racquets at small moving objects with deadly accuracy. I once read Bridget Jones's Diary, Captain Corelli's Mandolin and To Kill a Mockingbird in one afternoon and still had time to build a suspension bridge in my back garden before nightfall. The laws of physics do not apply to me. I balance, I weave, I dodge, I frolic and I pay my bills on time. On weekends, to reduce stress, I participate in full contact Origami. I breed prize-winning starfish. I won an Oscar the year Dame Judy Dench was not nominated. I play the Italian nose flute. I don't perspire. I suffer from an intense dislike of traffic wardens. I wonder who else is out there in cyberspace?

MR ROMANTIC

So here I am…and there are you…I'm in East Grinstead! Here are a few lines about me as I like to write…So wherever you may be…if a thought could take me there…to see the smile within your eyes and light the fire within your heart… it is my soulmate I seek and true love…and could it be you and I walking side by side…or am I being too romantic…too me…my true soulmate I hope shares similar beliefs and goals… and one who can run with champions…soar with the eagles…and love like Romeo and Juliet…who loves life…and who knows themselves for what they are …truly an unbeatable force so beautiful is the power of two together as one…so wherever you are in life, your growth, your personal expansion with others…if we are compatible on the majority of issues…then let's talk some more…there we can talk, philosophise on life, about each other, mellow with fine old spirits from a bottle, then, pause a little…as the golden Sun exits the blue skies, submerging under the seas… the air cools, the bottle runs dry, a different light appears….the Moon so bright, casting silhouettes of two on the sands, warm and comforting, waters glistening, a sense of tranquil [sic] emerges!!…if not and quote, c'est la vie, unquote (that's life) and good luck…fly well into the night…like the dove of peace to discover new lands….in the sea of life…go well my friend…go well….

YOUR SEXY LOVER 69

I am Indian male five foot eight inches tall, medium build dark hairs brown eyes olive skin with hairy chest singal with no ties 100% honest loving caring romantic horney sexy guy. My hobbies are:- reading tv music good food country-side walk travel good food with bottles of wine {WITH U LOVE} friend ship meeting new peoples many more. Extra hobbies are :- live life 2 full cinema comedy romance love sex cuddles hugs kisses…more? Love to meet gorgeous sexy romantic busty curvaceous large voluptuous [sic] lady of any AREA – age-size-WEIHGHT– height-COLOUR – with/out children. Life is too short come on honey let us have some good time before it is to late. If u are looking 4 causal - occacional sexy lover short – long trems- life partner. IF have been neglect by men & your partner 4 an reason & u have not getting what u need Any fantasies suggestion other offer also most welcome, please u can apply with full details WITH photo. Life is to have some fun, come to me we will have best time tighter darling. This offer is just 4 one week only, after that time my adds will end on this page. Just doont wait look around u. just send e mail to get more fun u wanted in your sexy funny time same day may be tonight. Thanks for reading this your fast response can't bring the best, who knoes our life will change bytonight darling. *[Author's note: I have not altered the spelling, but left it to stand in all its glory!]*

Quite apart from all the jokers and the crazies out there on the internet, is online dating for you? I would advise you not to rule it out, as there are a lot of genuine people just like you who would like a meaningful relationship.

Here are some tips from experts **Rosalind Sedacca and Amy Sherman** in their excellent book, **"Smart Dating Advice for Women Over 40: Answers to Your Most-Asked Questions"**. Pick up the e-book for free at http://www.womendatingafter40.com

Online dating is like learning a new language and can be intimidating or overwhelming at first. However, this is exciting territory for many boomers and certainly worth the effort. Just do your research and learn the basic dos and don'ts of effective online dating.

Understand the criteria for creating a good profile, for that is your calling-card. But also be cautious. Not everyone is playing by the same rules in cyberspace so proceed with maturity and wisdom. Schedule your first few dates during the daytime in places where you won't be alone. Coffee shops, parks, book stores and other public spaces are ideal for initial meetings.

Take things slowly and plan to have fun. You could be meeting a nice guy who shares your interests and values. Many successful relationships have started at online dating sites. So there's no reason to exclude a viable resource for meeting someone special. Just don't let romantic fantasy overrule your common sense.

When trying online dating, avoid these common mistakes:
1. *Do not reveal too much in your initial emails. In other words, do not write your whole life story. Let there be some mystery about you so when you finally meet, you'll have something to talk about.*
2. *Never lie about yourself. The truth will come out eventually and be likely to ruin the relationship at that point. So, admit your true age, use a recent picture and don't change your appearance so that your photo doesn't look like*

you. You're off to a bad start when someone is expecting you to look one way and sees you looking differently.

3. *Do not seem too eager or desperate because no one finds that attractive. Play it cool at first until you get to know your date better.*

Being part of a couple doesn't necessarily guarantee you happiness. You still have problems to deal with in life and I can tell you from bitter experience that it's a hell of a lot better to be alone and be the master-or mistress-of your own destiny than be with the wrong person just for the sake of not being alone. Don't assume that having a partner, or living with your child's co-parent, would make everything OK. I also believe that when you finally are happy and secure in your own company, as a single person, your chances are much higher of meeting the right person at that point. In my case, when I gave up being so frantic about wanting to be with someone, that's when my Mr Right showed up. I had finally reached the point where I had decided that maybe it wasn't going to happen, yet realising that if that were the case I would be perfectly fine.

CHAPTER TWELVE

HOW TO DECIDE IF HE'S RIGHT?

Creating the Perfect Partner List
Features of a Successful Relationship

Here's what you should look for:

- *You are able to be your authentic, natural self around him*
- *You treat each other equally, with one person not being more dominant or demanding*

- *You feel comfortable being open and honest*
- *You share similar values, philosophies and goals*
- *You respect each other without compromising who you are*
- *You are attracted to each other and are compatible in bed*
- *You allow each other time to pursue your own interests and also share many common activities*
- *You have fun together*
- *You handle disagreements respectfully and fairly*
- *Most of your time together is enjoyable and not filled with drama or despair*

Extract from "Smart Dating Advice for Women Over 40: Answers to Your Most-Asked Questions" by Rosalind Sedacca and Amy Sherman

Pick up the e-book for free at **http://www.womendatingafter40.com**

Debunking the most popular relationship myths
by Marina Pearson

MYTH: Love is only about support.

TRUTH: Love is a balance of support and challenge.

Love is about being supported and challenged at the same time. The love that we are sometimes exposed to in movies does not exist. That is definitely the fairy tale version. Love has both a negative and positive aspect to it. Now, I know that you are probably thinking "Marina, are you mad?" and my answer is "No".

I have lots of friends who have children and there are days their children really challenge them, and there are days that the kids behave themselves and are like angels. Do their parents love them? Sure they do. Are their kids sometimes challenging them and sometimes supporting them? Yes, they are. The same will go for your ex. He will challenge you and be supporting you at the same time. Love is about balance. If you were just supported all the time, you wouldn't grow or evolve. I know it's maybe tough to get your head around this, but by the end of the book you will understand what I mean.

MYTH: Relationships are all about happiness.

TRUTH: Relationships are also about growth, not only happiness.

Relationships are not only here to make you happy; they are here to make you grow and learn about who you are. This is crucial to understand. Why? Because if you are setting happiness as the benchmark for your relationship's success, you will feel very disappointed and wonder why relationships are hard or why they don't work. Because we all know that no one is happy in a relationship 100 per cent of the time.

However, if you set growth as a benchmark for your relationship's success, you will probably find that you have a lot of relationship success. As the old adage says: "If you are not growing, you are dying." So why not use this time to grow and evolve?

MYTH: Your partner in a happy relationship is committed to what is important to YOU!

TRUTH: Partners in a relationship are firstly committed to what is important to them and not to you.

People commit to relationships based on whether their values are being ticked or, even better, shared by their partner. If they feel that what is important to them is being supported, they will stay. If what is highly important to them is being challenged, they will either stray or leave permanently.

For example, if a man believes that his wife doesn't appreciate his financial contribution towards the family, or that she is being challenged by the fact he doesn't contribute enough to what she finds important (for instance, spending time with the family), then chances are one of them will stray, as neither is being appreciated for contributing to what the other finds important.

Being aware of these myths will help you understand what relationships are truly about. In this way your perspective will widen and unrealistic expectations will decrease, thereby lessening possible disappointment.

There are other myths besides the ones listed above, which are discussed in more detail during my Goodbye Mr Ex audio and video programmes.

7 key factors that keep you struggling

Aside from the myths, I have identified seven key things that women do, or don't do, that will keep them stuck in the pain and anger, stopping them from moving on.

I have found that when my clients either come to me or the workshops I have hosted, they are in the struggle because:

they are not committed to letting go—they would prefer to be right and hang onto their fears;

they judge themselves and their ex, which keeps them angry and jealous;

they re-hash the same story over and over, which renders them powerless and keeps them obsessing;

they make massive assumptions about their ex and hold unrealistic expectations, which keeps them disappointed and frustrated;

they use language that blames and shames their ex, which keeps them in the conflict with their ex and themselves;

they keep wishing they had done things differently, which keeps them in guilt and are very worried about what will happen in the future, which keeps them in the fear; and/or

they surround themselves with the wrong support, either because they falsely believe that family and friends are the best people to talk to, or they seek no outside support as they believe that doing it on their own will be just fine.

Can you identify with any of these behaviours above?

Marina Pearson is an inspirational speaker, bestselling author and the founder of Divorce Shift, an organization that supports women who are struggling to get over their ex relationships, to leave them feeling like the best thing since sliced bread. She has been featured in the UK newspapers such as The Guardian and The Daily Mail, and in Marie Claire, Best, Now, Spirit & Soul, MSN HER, while being featured in women's magazines discussing matters of divorce and her own journey. She is also a prolific blogger for The Huffington Post, Eharmony and YourTango.

Learn how to get over your ex for free: www.DivorceShift.com/GoodbyeMrEx

Download your free chapters: www.GoodbyeMrEx.com

Emer I just got married last year. I don't know if I ever saw myself as a lone parent, more of a single parent, a very stubbornly single parent for many years, and when I met my husband a couple of years ago he had a very hard time getting me to let go—not of my independence, but to let him in because I was extremely focused on the bubble of me and my daughter—our place, our life, her school and everything. So it took a little bit of work to begin with but it's great now. I met him because he was part of the same friends group in Brighton and he was actually sharing a house with my daughter's dad at the time when we started going out! I've known him for about five or six years. We were friends but we didn't get together for a couple of years. As soon as we started going out we obviously checked that it was OK with my ex. He was truly happy and encouraging because he really likes my husband. I remember seeing him with my daughter when I was over at their house and being really impressed with how great he was with her. That was obviously an initial attraction point as well. He moved out straight away so that we could see how it would go and he was quite eager! He proposed within ten months. It was quite difficult for him initially because he was coming in. I It took him a while to understand how it was with my daughter, and also to understand her limitations and capabilities. I think he found it hard with the Downs Syndrome to work out what was my daughter being slightly lazy and what was her just not being able to do it. It took a good while of that first year of living together for him to understand, because I was so used to what she was, and wasn't able to do. So it wasn't a normal situation for him to step in to—not only going out with somebody with a child but also one with a disability, and having to deal with that. Now it's great, but it was pretty difficult in the beginning for everyone to adjust to it. I think him being so good with my daughter is definitely a major part of it...

Annabel *Anyone in a good relationship will tell you: to some extent it is luck—some work, some don't. Maybe it isn't all about your judgement, maybe when you first meet people they're not really what you think because they're trying to make a good impression on you.*

When you fall in love with someone you are also, to some extent, projecting onto them all your hopes and dreams and fantasies of what true love is. I wanted to make a go of it in my first marriage but I remember a good friend of mine pointing out that it didn't say very much for my self-esteem if I was prepared to accept his betrayal of me and as my sister said, in the end it might just prove too hard suppressing all my anger about what he'd done. In the end I had no choice anyway because he made the decision, not me. It was probably just as well things didn't work out, from that point of view. I would always have felt like second best and my current husband treats me like the best thing ever. You've got to be the most important person to them—it's got to be a proper and equal partnership, otherwise: what's it all for? You've already proved that you can survive as a single mother and look after the children by yourself. So how can you tell if he's Mr. Right and worth giving up your freedom for?

I kept my original perfect partner list that I wrote all those years ago. Among other things, I was looking for someone tall, dark and handsome (sometimes clichés are created with good reason!), solvent, ambitious and honourable. It was important to me that he got on well with my children, family and friends and also my dog (more of this later), that he had a sense of humour, could make me laugh and was someone I really enjoyed talking to. I wanted him to be intelligent, compassionate and kind. You may find it strange and unrealistic that I chose to be so specific. When I met and fell in love with my second husband I convinced myself that my list was overambitious as it emerged that he did not tick every box. Indeed, the more I came to know about him, the more apparent this became.

One of the things from the list that stood out from the start was that he did not like my dog. She was old and decrepit by the time he met her and (although I did not realise this at the time) increasingly blind. As a result of this she often did not get out of the way in time and he was forever tripping over her and cursing her for being so annoying. I began to suspect that he might have done more than shout at her but I couldn't prove it. The boys and I always stood up for her and did our best to make it up to her, but over time she became very nervous and wary around him, which upset me as she was our beloved old friend, a loyal family pet who'd been endlessly sweet and patient with the children as they grew older. I tried to rationalise the situation, reasoning that it wasn't the end of the world if my husband didn't like the dog. After all, she was clearly nearing the end of her life and I'd make sure she was alright. But it still troubled me and I had a nagging feeling that something was amiss. However, life had become very difficult then as he became increasingly moody and I was pre-occupied with a situation at home that became more and more confusing and unhappy, so I went into survival mode once more and switched my attention to trying to find a solution to my husband's erratic and aggressive behaviour.

However, I have always been haunted by guilt that my dog didn't have a better time in the remaining years of her life, and I've since realised that his cruelty towards an innocent and harmless animal was a warning bell. I should have paid attention sooner to the clues. I have subsequently realised the danger of not listening to my intuition and the memory of my dog Pepper will help me to do that in future.

A footnote to this story is that when I met my current husband I realised that here *was* someone who ticked all the boxes on my list, so I was glad that I'd had the courage to ask for exactly what I wanted (indeed I wished that I hadn't compromised with my disastrous second marriage–all I needed to do was to wait patiently until the real Mr Right showed up, instead of making do with Mr Mostly Wrong!) Over the years I have learnt a lot about visualising and goal setting and I now know that whilst you should be realistic, you should also be specific. Why don't you try it now? Start with the words: *My Perfect Partner is:* …and write down everything that comes to mind. Don't worry too much about putting the "right" things down to begin with, just go with the flow. You can always edit it later and when you have the final version that you are happy with, write your list out neatly, adding doodles, colours or decorations if you like. Then put it somewhere safe and refer to it when you need inspiration or clarification. There's nothing to stop you changing your mind and editing it later, but beware of altering it to better fit someone who, you already know, at some level is not right for you.

Louise *The reason I tried so hard to make it work with my second husband is that I wanted the "family unit"; I wanted them to have the male role model that they hadn't had with their own dad and it should have been ideal but it wasn't. It was the right sentiment but the wrong person! I didn't have the warning signs but it all happened too soon. If I hadn't agreed to get married so quickly those signs would have become apparent over a period of time.*

There's a good reason for that saying "Marry in haste, repent at leisure"! If it's that good it doesn't matter if you wait a little longer–you've got the rest of your lives, after all.

Louise *If somebody came to me now and said "I've fallen in love and I want to get married", I would certainly advise them to wait a while. If it's going to go wrong anyway, the longer you leave it to be on the safe side, the better. Don't ask me how to tell if he's right –God, no! I wouldn't be able to comment on that! I even wrote a list before I met 'B**tard Number 2'and he ticked all the boxes. I was having lunch with a friend one day and we jokingly wrote out the list. One of the boxes was solvent (tick), one was good with children (tick) and before we got married, he was. He had two sons himself and he had managed as a single father. I thought he would understand. It was only after we got married I realised the huge cracks in his relationship with his <u>own</u> sons. Then he started ignoring <u>my </u>son. At one point before we got married he'd asked a builder for a quote to extend the house, so my daughter* *could have had her own room, as she'd had before. I said to him that my daughter had waited a long time for a bedroom of her own, and needed one as 'she was hitting that age'. But then suddenly that wasn't happening any more. Everything changed. I couldn't even paint the kid's bedroom and toys were not allowed outside of their room. We were just like lodgers. It wasn't a home.*

Take your time and get to know your new partner very well before introducing them to your child of any age. Children are emotionally vulnerable when new adults enter their lives, especially when they're dating their mother. Don't create a revolving door of "new friends" for your children to meet. Wait until you know this is a very special friend worthy of their attention. And then take it very slowly.

Make sure you remind your children that no one will ever replace their "real" (Mom or) Dad (unless you are justified in doing so). The transitions are a lot smoother when the new "friend" doesn't come across as a new "parent".

Even older, grown children need a transition period to accept a new partner in your life. Talk to them, acknowledge their feelings and allegiance to their father. Don't "push" a new date on them. Remember, it's your life, but having the support of your adult children is certainly a wonderful asset!

Extract from "Smart Dating Advice for Women Over 40: Answers to Your Most-Asked Questions" by Rosalind Sedacca and Amy Sherman.

Pick up the e-book for free at **http;//www.womendatingafter40.com**

Louise *Your children have to know that they can express their feelings and their thoughts about this person because children are very loyal. When you have them going off to visit their father, they won't say some of the things they perhaps should say because they don't want to hurt you, and they might not talk to him about things for the same reason. Kids can get very confused as to what they can say. If they can see that you're happy they might conceal their opinion, so they need to know they can say something without fear of reprisal. Again, with time it should become obvious how your child is feeling and coping with your new relationship. Yet again, time is the answer.*

If I hadn't rushed into marriage then these problems would inevitably have shown themselves. I think in hindsight two years is about the right amount of time to really get to know someone.

I heartily agree with this. In a period of two years it's impossible for someone to keep up an act. In those two years you have to have had enough contact with a potential partner in all sorts of situations, good and bad. I think you definitely should have been on at least one holiday, (preferably a family holiday!) so you can really see how that person reacts in all those different circumstances before you make a judgement about them, because initially they will only be showing you their best side. Time apart to reflect is also a good idea because if you spend every minute of the day together, you don't get that. So you need to keep that little bit of space that's just for you, particularly for your children, because he might be the answer to all *your* dreams but he might **not** be the answer to all *their* dreams. You've therefore got to make sure that you have a bubble where you as the original family unit can still interact and you can check how your children are feeling about it all. I suppose if you are able to meet this person's family and friends on a regular basis, you should also learn a lot about them. My second husband was always very reticent about this. I never met his parents (he excused this by saying that as they were both alcoholics they'd only be an embarrassment, and he'd fallen out with them now anyway). I met his children. I met one sister and her husband but not his other two siblings. His best friend was "too busy" to come to our wedding and besides, it was such a long way away from where they all lived…it was just excuse after excuse. He spun so many tales and made up so many excuses but he was so plausible and I was way too trusting. I was in love; I wanted to believe he was a good man who'd had a tough start in life. At first I really believed his story of the pot of gold at the end of the rainbow. It was only at the end that I saw it for the crock of b******t that it really was! Remember the old adage that actions speak louder than words, in so many ways. There was always an excuse for all the bad stuff that happened. I would encourage anybody who is unsure of a prospective partner to look at the facts as *you* see them, not as he is dressing them up.

Louise *Everything was a lie before we got married. We couldn't even pass an Estate Agent's window without him looking for "a house big enough for six". So before we got married he was showing me that he was willing to provide a home for all of us, and yet when we got married I discovered that he was actually not prepared to move out of his house at all. I had two cats, and to begin with he said "Well, there's no way they're going in the bedroom". This was fine, because his house* *had a door that would keep them out, but as soon as we moved in, they were put out in the conservatory, which was freezing, and weren't allowed in the house at all. It was just so horrible that after two weeks I started looking for a better home for them. So, again, all of those things would have come out if I'd waited. He was so false to everybody. In some respects he was similar to my first husband, who'd put on this bravado of "life is great and this latest deal is going to come off". (Deluded). I also used to think what a perfect marriage he'd had with his previous wife, and what a perfect life they'd had, and it was later that his eldest son said to me one day "Did you know that Mum and Dad were getting a divorce before she died?" That one sentence just blew away his picture of perfect wife, perfect life and so many things that he had said before; I now understood. Time will unveil all the inconsistencies. I think when you meet somebody new you don't want to continually talk about the past, but on some level you do have to find out, certainly in order to decide if you have a future together. I do remember the passion and the intensity and how you just don't want to be apart, but logically after 6 months that level of passion subsides and then a different kind of love comes in. So you need to stand back again when that happens.*

You have to work out for yourself if there's a running theme of why all their (or your) past relationships have failed. Anyone can be unlucky, or make a mistake, but there might be something in what they're not telling you. I'm not telling you to be paranoid, I'm just encouraging you to keep your wits about you. It is also wise to ensure that you have thoroughly explored what went wrong in your last serious relationship and the part you played. Any old issues should be resolved before you start again with someone new. If you need help, speak to a trained professional.

HELP AND HEALING TIPS

If, like me you have become haunted by a wrong or limiting decision you made, or a negative emotion such as guilt, fear or anger I would strongly recommend going to see a Beyond NLP practitioner. There are two wonderful processes that your practitioner can take you through, called the Decision Destroyer and the Emotion Obliterator. With the help of an expert you will be able to release events and emotions which have traumatised or held you back and move forward free of these particular obstacles to your wholeness and happiness.

For details of your local practitioner, please see the list at the end of the book. Alternatively, send an email to **vivienne@thelifeyoudeserve.co.uk** and I will forward you the contact details of someone who will be able to help you.

Choosing a new partner when you have kids already from a previous relationship means that you have to be extra vigilant not to repeat your own past mistakes–or make a whole load of new ones! Your kids are depending on you to get it right.

"There is a high percentage of failed second marriages and you don't want to make the same mistakes twice. Be aware of the following guidelines before you make another commitment:

1. *Be comfortable discussing money issues because financial problems are a big concern after you are married. How a couple deals with those issues can make or break a relationship.*
2. *If communication is a problem before marriage, you know you will have difficulties after marriage. Therefore, be available to discuss things openly and regularly for your marriage to work.*
3. *Step-children, in-laws, your children, etc. may become sources of problems in a new marriage. Be sensitive to these family issues so you can work them out.*
4. *Sexual incompatibility, including frequency and quality, is often a common reason for divorce. Explore all aspects of intimacy before tying the knot.*
5. *Be aware of any addictions to drugs or alcohol, as either will make any relationship impossible. Never ignore your suspicions.*
6. *Do not tolerate any verbal abuse and certainly no physical abuse. Abusive behaviour always increases after marriage, as the abuser feels entitled to his behavior.*

If you are having concerns about any of the above, seek out professional guidance together. Many challenges can be handled through therapy or by learning more effective communication skills. If you're not feeling comfortable after working with an outside expert, that may be the time to reconsider this relationship–before it's too late!"

Extract from "Smart Dating Advice for Women Over 40: Answers to Your Most-Asked Questions" by Rosalind Sedacca and Amy Sherman

Annabel *And as soon as I met him I felt this incredible sense of attraction, but also belonging. I felt safe. My first husband is very attractive, a real smoothie. But he never looked after me. He just treated me like a wife. Before we got engaged I overheard a conversation between my ex and his college friends where he said "I think I'm going to ask her to marry me; I think she'll be good wife material." It sounded so cold and I remember how upset I was at the time. I should have pulled the plug then, but it's easy to say that now. Love is blind, as they say. This time round it's completely different. My husband says "My job is to look after you." And it's really sweet because that's what he does. He tells me he loves me 25 times a day, still—and we've been married two and a half years. I never had any of that in my first marriage. It was hard to realise how much stuff I'd done before and been unappreciated for. I think I became a bit of a doormat, and that's really funny because that's **so** not me! I had metamorphosed into this different person.*

Helen *Then I went out one night on my birthday and he was there (he was a friend of a friend). I knew he was right because of his relationship with his mother. Sometimes I wish he would do more with the kids but he's got this thing that because they're girls and he's a man…and of course they're not his own. Had he been their natural father then I'm sure their relationship would have been different. But he's helpful to me. Don't expect too much. In a way I think I'm probably still the boss with the kids and I always will be. Although I do let him have his say—you've got to do that and you've got to let them discipline the children if you are in agreement with each other, but if I don't agree with him I will say. The children have always come first, always will. Even if I was still with their natural father, they would still come first (whereas some people say "Ooh no—my husband comes before my children"). The kids are your own flesh and blood, after all! And my husband knew that from the word go.*

I agree—if one of my kids is really unhappy or in trouble, whatever age they are, sorting that out will always be my first priority and luckily that's one of the things my husband understands and loves about me. There's a wonderful saying which I subscribe to, which is: "You're only as happy as your unhappiest child".

CHAPTER THIRTEEN

DEALING WITH THE CHALLENGES OF BLENDED FAMILIES

Successfully Stepping From Being a Single Mum to Creating a Blended Family With a New Partner

Annabel *I also sometimes really wish that my children had a better father, you know? I look at other people who have really nice, close parents and I think how brilliant it is for the children to be brought up in that environment. We don't have that and we'll never have that "whole family" thing. Even though my second husband is really good with them, they're not his children, in the same way that his aren't mine and we will never be able to recreate that unit because there's always a little bit of friction there, especially as they're getting older now. They're looking at him and they're thinking "You can't tell me what to do" and you know, he's a good stepfather, so what must it be like for people whose new partners don't try so hard? It must be horrendous.*

Maggie *My children had such a hard time coping with my ex when we got together. They really played up and we had tantrums and scenes on a regular basis. He was very opinionated and was always telling me to be tougher on them, but I was in two minds, really. I hated him telling them off and of course he wasn't their real Dad, so I could sort of see their point that he shouldn't be telling them what to do. In the end I went to see my doctor, who basically said that it was his responsibility as an adult to **be** the adult and that he should let me carry on enforcing the house rules we'd always had. He could support me, but otherwise he should try and stay out of any squabbles.*

When it came to my second husband's children, I also found it very tricky. His son was in his twenties and I got on with him very well. His daughter, however, was quite a challenge, to put it mildly! I remember that the first time I met her she kept calling me by his previous girlfriend's name. The first couple of times I thought it must have been a mistake but then I realised it was quite deliberate. We'd be walking down the street and she'd walk just in front of me, so I kept stumbling. I recall one lunch where she sat through the whole meal with her back to me, which I found incredibly rude! We had this nightmare weekend, where we hired a remote cottage beside a Scottish Loch. My ex was a very impatient driver and it was an eleven hour drive; my job was to keep the kids quiet and entertained, so that they wouldn't "distract" him—I was by now beginning to anticipate his temper outbursts and do my best to divert them. I saw the weekend as a great opportunity to aid the process of blending our two families together. We stopped to pick up his son and daughter and made our way to the cottage, getting lost several times but finally arriving after a very fraught trip. Every time I spoke to his daughter, picked a piece of music to listen to in the car or just made a suggestion she would fold her arms, stare defiantly at me and simply say 'No!' or 'You're weird!' It was Halloween, so I nearly bust a gut sourcing the ingredients for a special meal, decorating the cottage with witches, ghosts, bats and cobwebs, baking a themed cake, thinking of games etc. but nothing would thaw my step-daughter's icy demeanour. She told off my son for not playing hide-and-seek according to her rules and sulked for hours when she didn't get her way. My ex picked a quarrel with his son over something minor and it rained and rained. My favourite part of the weekend was a precious hour alone walking on the banks of the loch and admiring the ruins of an old castle. His daughter never did soften towards me and on the rare occasion when her Dad noticed how insolent she was being towards me he never reprimanded her, explaining that he saw her rarely enough and he was scared of alienating her because he'd messed up so much already with her upbringing. I did understand this, but it didn't make my job any easier trying to prove I wasn't the "Wicked Step-mother"!

I now have two new stepchildren. I don't see them more than about three times a year, as they live in East Germany and they hardly speak any English. Here again I recognise that I must be patient, lower my expectations and try just to be a benign and friendly presence. Most of the time this works quite well (especially when I use my secret weapon, drawing, and get them colouring in one of my designs) but even then I have my moments when it all seems impossibly hard. I recall one trip in particular where I had spent weeks memorising German vocabulary, so as to be able to communicate better. When we checked in to our self-catering apartment I realised I might have a challenge to create appetising meals for our four children in a kitchen that was literally the dimensions of a small cupboard. To top it all, I was suffering from acute cystitis and the doctor's surgery was closed over the weekend in the remote winter sport resort where we were staying! I must confess I had a meltdown moment when my small step-son refused to take my hand in order to cross the main road. He also had the mother of all tantrums, causing his sister to glare at me reproachfully and random passers-by to throw curious looks our way (do I really look like a child abductor?!) I the end I thrust my screaming step-son at his Dad and stomped off to the nearest park, muttering to myself about ingratitude–"After all I've done!" I know of course that the unreasonable behaviour is mine. It's confusing for children to adapt to new arrangements and it's not surprising that they often resent a new adult in their lives. Who can blame them, really? And far be it from me to demand their trust and friendship before they are ready to give it. It's a gradual process and all the more rewarding for that. I remember reading that, as a step-parent, the most you can hope is for your step-kids to see you as a friendly figure in their lives. The most you can expect is to develop a mutual liking for each other. Love may come, but only if you are really lucky. My two boys adore my (current) husband-and he them-and we never stop counting our blessings about that.

Belinda and Simon It's probably self-evident, but every blended family situation is unique, and there is no single pathway to success. Nevertheless, there are some key guiding principles which seem likely to have applicability to most, if not all, blended families—and this is what we have pulled together below.

It's worth bearing in mind that many of these guiding principles are equally relevant to non-blended families. They are, essentially, about "good parenting". It's just that blended family situations expose any flaws and limitations (which we all have!) to a greater degree.

And when we talk about "success", this certainly doesn't mean that there will not be great challenges and difficult problems to face. It's how these are handled that probably makes the difference.

In our narrative below, we are describing blended family situations where one of the birth parents and his/her children are joined by a new partner. This is the most common scenario. But, of course, there are situations where there are 2 groups of children to be integrated into the new family—which seems likely to make it even more important to agree, and adopt, some very clear guiding principles from the outset.

Some Guiding Principles

These guiding principles are not set out in any particular order of priority—as some will have a greater relevance to a particular situation than others. So, in a sense, it's a "checklist" to assist blended families (or those considering becoming one) to ensure that as many angles as possible are covered as they enter a new, and crucially important, phase of their lives.

1. *Spend as much time as possible before moving in together. Don't rush it! Use this time to gradually begin the blending process, and to discuss and agree the guiding principles that will underpin all that follows. [This should include money matters].*

2. *As soon as possible after the decision to blend, find a way of creating a new home environment so that ownership of the living space is shared and equal.*

3   *Where the other birth parent is around, create a positive environment, and plentiful opportunities, for him or her to be involved, and have individual time, with the children. And ensure that good and open communication is established between all involved.*

4. *t's very important that the new partner does not try and be a substitute father/mother figure if the other birth parent is around and involved. Be careful about the use of the term "step-parent" in these circumstances, as it may heighten the conflict of loyalties which the children will anyway be feeling.*

5. *The 2 adults in the blended family need to agree where responsibility will lie for "discipline" and key decision-making with regards to the children. Almost certainly this should, in the early days at least, lie with the birth parent in the blended family, as the children are unlikely to accept this from the new partner.*

6. *The 2 adults also need to share a common set of ethical and moral values— especially in relation to parenting. This may sound high-minded (and, of course can be rather intangible), but unless there are consistent messages on these key issues, the children will be confused, and (being children!) are likely to play the adults off against each other.*

7. *It's important that the birth parent in the newly blended family spends ample individual time with his / her own children. As most of them will have experienced this as part of a single-parent family, they will feel a sense of loss and resentment if their birth-parent now turns all her / his attention to the new partner. This can be hard on the new partner – so this needs to be taken into account, too.*

8. *Where possible, the adults in the blended family should try and establish a process for resolving the inevitable conflicts that will arise between them (however smart they think they've been in agreeing the guiding principles!)–a process that should at all times avoid involving, or upsetting, the children.*

9. *There needs to be sensitivity to the significance of changing the birth parent's, or children's, surname. Names are vital to our sense of identity, and it may well be wise to keep them as they are!*

10. *And connected to this, it would also seem important not to change the children's schools, or friendship groups-especially during the earlier stages of the blended family journey. The children will have enough on their plates without moving them away from other familiar and stabilising situations and relationships.*

"My parents divorced when I was young but I was brought up in two really loving households. I didn't have a contentious relationship with my mom or dad."

— Matt Damon

"You do need parental guidance and I was in a great position with both my mum and dad. They split when I was a baby but even though I stayed with my mom they were both very much involved in my upbringing."

— Leonardo DiCaprio

CHAPTER FOURTEEN

BEING CONTENTEDLY SINGLE

Celebrating Your Achievements

"It is of practical value to learn to like yourself. Since you must spend so much time with yourself you might as well get some satisfaction out of the relationship."

—Norman Vincent Peale

I know for a lot of single mums it's a case of "No! I don't want to be on my own. How will I cope?" But it is perfectly possible, indeed an extremely understandable and valid choice to make, to stay on your own–or even to determine that you will do all that it takes to achieve that contentment and happiness on your own even if ultimately you are seeking another partner. Because one thing's for sure-and this I tell you from heartfelt experience–there's nothing more lonely than being in a relationship just for the sake of not being alone; being in the wrong relationship with the wrong person is far worse than being contentedly single, with choices and options open to you. Stay true to your authentic self and find peace in your own company, before you rush into giving up that hard-won peace and equilibrium for just anybody. It may just be that, like Angela and Elaine, you discover that contented singlehood is actually a life-enhancing choice that brings you to a new level of happiness and acceptance.

"Independence is happiness."

—Susan B. Anthony

"The secret to happiness is freedom... And the secret to freedom is courage."

—Thucydides

Is it Really OK to be Single?
By Francine Kay

That's an interesting question for many of us who are single. And the fact is that if it's not OK and you are single, resisting your reality can impact your life negatively. If you are single right now you may see this as a temporary time in your life. Perhaps, for all kinds of reasons, you may have resigned yourself to it. Or, being single right now might be very liberating, relaxing and enjoyable.

If you are single right now it's normal to experience lonely feelings, hopeless feelings, and anxious feelings at times. It's just as normal to experience feelings of contentedness, peace and ease. Although you may be aware of what you are experiencing physically, mentally and on an emotional level, no one teaches us how to be Consciously Single. That means specific ways to accept and embrace your single status as equally as valid as being in a relationship.

How Do I Do 'Being Single'?

In my Contented Singles Programme, I explain that there is a skill in the actual "doing" and "being" of single.

What Does Being Single Mean to You?

Answer these questions to give yourself some insight:

Could you have dinner in a restaurant, a drink in a bar, or going to a show or the movies alone?

Are you annoyed by single supplements in hotels or do you understand the logic behind it?

Do you believe that it's just as true to say that being in a couple, especially when you are not happy, can be equally as challenging as being single?

Would you compromise your personal values to be in a relationship?

There is a very simple way to put your challenges around being single into a perspective that empowers you rather than deflates you. It's not anything new or unique, in fact every leader in the field of personal development and all the advances in neuro sciences agree on this very idea. It's simply this: Change your thoughts. If you keep your challenging thoughts at the front of your mind, guess what? Being single will appear to be challenging. Makes sense, doesn't it? So how do you put it into action? The most important thing to know is that your every thought will define the quality of your life on a minute-by-minute and hour-by-hour basis. This means you firstly have to get very conscious of your thoughts. For every challenging thought, counteract it by firstly acknowledging it. In your mind say "yes, and another way of thinking about it is..." and find a happier perspective. I have clients do this repeatedly. I show them diagrams that help them remember how to do this. Some of them even wear elastic bands on their wrists that they ping, every time they catch their challenging thoughts, to remind themselves to find their new, happier thoughts. The truth is that you are where you are right now until you are not. There are two ways of being single. One is accepting. The other is resisting. You will always know which camp you are in by the quality of your thoughts. So you can have this be easy or hard, and ultimately the choice is yours. And unless you "choose" to be single when you are single, your resistance will lead to unhappiness.

The Concept of Self Love and How to Apply It

We've not been taught to be selfish. We have been taught to put others first. Part of being consciously and contentedly single is to put yourself first. Imagine getting up at the weekend with two days of freedom in front of you. Ask yourself: What would I enjoy doing today? What would light me up? What would be good for me? What would make me feel happy?

Once you get into the habit of putting yourself first and really knowing what is important to your personal happiness, you'll find that even in another relationship you are able to independently make yourself happy. Understanding this concept means that you are capable of self-love and not looking to your partner to provide all your happiness. That's far too big a demand and anyway, it's not their job. Your happiness is an inside job. Any new partner that comes along is an enhancement to your already contented life.

Added Extras for the Contented Single

- *Develop and sustain a good relationship network of friends, family and mentors*
- *Protect your health*
- *Take the time to work on you to understand who you are and how you react and behave in relationships. This is a crucial part of my Contented Singles programme. It's vital to understand the role you play in relationships, how your past may still be impacting your present and how to avoid repeating old patterns in the future.*
- *Ultimately become a Conscious and Contented Single who chooses her life in or out of a relationship.*

Francine Kaye: As one of the most experienced relationship coaches in the UK, Francine is the relationship expert for the Channel 5 programme The Wright Stuff appears on The Trisha Show, The Vanessa Show, The Gaby Logan Show and GMTV and is featured in and writes for national magazines, the press and is a guest on national radio. She is invited for her expertise on BBC, CNN, 5Live, Nick Ferrari, Vanessa Feltz, Jumoke Fashola, Paul Ross, Lowrie Turner and many others.

Francine is also the author of "The Divorce Doctor" published by Hay House and "Time to Live" published by Hodder, and is an expert

workshop leader and trainer. Francine has her own weekly radio show on Glastonbury Radio.

Her experience as a Counsellor, Relationship Coach, Parent Effectiveness Trainer, Non Violent Communication Coach, Family Mediator, Family Consultant, Imago Clinical Therapist and NLP Practitioner qualifies her to help men and women find and sustain fulfilling relationships, help couples rebuild and redesign rocky relationships and, in cases where divorce is the only prognosis, she gives her clients the skills and strategies to do what it takes to Divorce with Dignity and heal their hearts and their lives. Francine also has a corporate side to her business and works with The Lloyds TSB Network, Shell, BP, Nokia, Tesco, Marks and Spencer and BMW as a trainer and workshop presenter.

Divorced 17 years ago with two small children, Francine has experienced the challenges of an uncertain future as a single parent. She has overcome financial adversity and in the past years has transformed her life to become one of the UK's most successful relationship coaches. Francine says, "As a direct result of accepting my new life instead of resisting it, I have regained my identity, healed my heart and learned to love again, and now I am helping others to do the same."

T: 020 8416 0121 E: francine@francinekaye.com www.francinekaye.com

Angela A year and a half after my ex-husband left, I was out dancing with my friend (we used to go out dancing every week) and somehow I ended up with John! I don't know what happened this one night-I just ended up with John! Then he'd phone and we talked and talked. He was fifteen years younger than I was and we were shocked because we didn't think that would be the case. I wasn't going to see him any more, but he was just so nice. I was thinking, if I was going to describe John, it was like being enveloped in this strong sense of safety with this quiet persona—non-judgmental, and he just let me be who I was. We were totally free to be within the relationship. He treated me like I was the most beautiful person on earth, which my husband had not done. He did so much, he took me to places I'd never been, that my husband had not taken me to; he took me to the fireworks…he was phenomenal in my life. He actually died the day after my ex got married last summer. I had broken up with him two years before that. So we were just over five years together. I broke up with him because I was so busy doing my Masters and I said "It's not you–I just don't want to be with anyone where I have to show up or explain myself. I raised four kids, I was married for thirty years, I just want to be free to go off, if I want to go to Hawaii, just to go off and not be in any relationship." But we did speak every week on the phone after that and actually I had just spoken to him a few days before he passed away. Oh my god, that was another devastating loss when he was gone. So that's it, really. Those are the two main men in my life! Now I could go on a motorcycle ride up to Whistler, just because I wanted to go on the back of a motorcycle, I took flying lessons—I've done everything that I've wanted to do. It's been phenomenal. I'm older though, you see…I'm 62 and so many women I know in this age group just have so much fun. We laugh and have a blast and our lives are just joyful! We say "Why would we want a man?" especially as we know so many women who are hooking up with men and all they're doing is just getting sick, and now they have to look after these men. It's kind of a crazy time in your life where you can just do what you want and you're not trying to get approval or please a man or anything!

Elaine I have to say that being here in this village has been the perfect place. I've also got some core friends from years ago (before I even had the children) and I think that's why I've been happy to stay on my own—not that I've ever met anyone that would make me want to change my mind—because I have a busy social life, lots of lovely friends, people to go on holiday with and at the moment I've no real reason to crave another partner, whereas I know some people cannot stand being on their own. So I suppose the knack of it is that I'm happy with what I've got; I've always got things going on at the weekend, so I don't find that a problem.

*I really could not envisage living with anybody else now. I'm not saying I wouldn't like to have somebody to go out with, go on holiday with, spend a weekend with, but actually **living with** somebody? I don't think I could do it now! I'm too set in my ways.*

I feel I can choose what I want to do now and this time is my time now. Actually, I'm rarely on my own for long, There'll be stretches of about four weeks at the most when I don't see either of the children. I work full time and have plenty of activities on in the evenings. I've got various friends that I see and go away with, so I'm quite comfortable. I would say also that I would be very wary of introducing somebody else into the family; that's easy for me to say because I was never in the position to do so, but at the back of my mind, after the rocky start that the children had, I would be extremely wary of introducing different people into the mix. I think the kids can see that I'm quite comfortable, but they've both been in steady relationships and I think they'd like to see me settle down again with someone. I guess there's a slight sense of them feeling: "Well, we've left Mum on her own now and it would be nice to know that there was someone else around now."

I do feel it's a real achievement to have raised happy and productive people in our children and we should applaud ourselves and each other for the milestones we reach in parenting.

"Everything I am is because of my mom."

— Sarah Michelle Gellar

"My mom is the backbone not just of my family but of many families."

— Shia LaBeouf

CHAPTER FIFTEEN

HAPPY EVER AFTER?

Moving On

"You build on failure. You use it as a stepping stone. Close the door on the past. You don't try to forget the mistakes, but you don't dwell on it. You don't let it have any of your energy, or any of your time, or any of your space."

—Johnny Cash

"Every day is a new day, and you'll never be able to find happiness if you don't move on."

—Carrie Underwood

Andrea *I was always very close to my husband's mother and before she died I talked to her about him wanting his mum to meet his new partner. But I was surprised and hurt by how quickly that all happened and by the fact that she liked her! Because people move on, I suppose, and I know that my husband used to say to her, people change. But I'd always thought that I'd stay married, that if we had a problem we'd deal with it, but we'd always be married. I married for life and I was always quite old-fashioned that way, perhaps because my own parents split up and I never wanted that for my children. I took them both to look round university and when the time came, I took them there. I kind of felt "Ok, you're paying for it and that's your contribution, but you lost the right to be involved in occasions like this". I guess it might have been different if he'd really been interested or determined to be a part of their education but he never seemed to pay much attention—too preoccupied with his new life, I guess. I cried my eyes out when my daughter left home to go to University and then she and I took my son when it was his turn. We left him in his halls of residence and went back and sat in the car, took one look at each other and cried our eyes out! She's like me, like a second mum to him in some ways. He's like his dad, I suppose—very soft and easy-going but he does stand up for himself when it matters. And now my grandson's the apple of my eye and my daughter's such a good mother and amazingly supportive to her partner. They're such great kids and I'm so proud of how they've both turned out. And me? I've become much tougher, I suppose after what happened to us. I don't talk about it much now and if I say something now, the children get really uppity with me: "Yes, we know, Mum. Move on! It's years ago now!"*

Angela *I believe in laughter. I've got a philosophy now in life which is that if it's not fun I don't do it, and I've really learnt to let go. Learn how to let go of and edit out negativity in your life so that being positive becomes normal. My expectations are limitless: that's my mantra really, so it's about being open and letting those good things come into your life. We're so good at giving graciously, it's also important to be able to receive gifts graciously as well. I'm completely grateful for my family and my friends. My eldest daughter now says "I wouldn't have changed any of our family experiences* *because that's what makes us the people we are". We're all who we are because of what we've gone through; we're all very empathetic, compassionate and forgiving people and really every experience you go through in life is the making of you.*

Louise *So, I suppose somewhere along the line I've done a good job, with the immense help of my family, even though I haven't got everything right. Somewhere along the line I did OK. Despite the most horrendous stuff that's been thrown at us we have survived. Just always make sure that the kids are alright, no matter what.*

Emer*. That's what got me out of being a flaky art student, the fact that I had this focus and it pushed me massively through life, and I'm extremely proud of everything that I've achieved. I've got my two degrees and I've got my MA and my post grad and now my teacher qualification and a good job. If I hadn't had my daughter, none of that would have happened. Definitely not. I would be backpacking round Australia, working on some banana farm or something!*

Over the last couple of years I've looked back on the situation and it was massive to be a single mum with a special needs child, but I think because I was young and I didn't know any different I just kind of clicked into it, and she was my main focus. It's amazing how you just do it, just get on with it. I think my success lies in not wallowing and not allowing myself to look at my situation in a negative way. Looking back on it now, though, I can understand people's reactions, because sometimes when people hear my story they think "I can't even look after myself, how could you look after your daughter and her disability?" but I think when you're a mum you just assume the responsibility and you just get on with it. And she's also just great—everyone who's met her thinks she's the bee's knees! She is a really special, amazing little girl that makes it so much easier, and she's a delight to be around.

Rachel *I am proud of keeping my head above water, helping my child to fulfil his potential despite having no assistance from his father. Remember it is not possible to do everything well, and it is possible to delegate stuff to others to save you time. Do the things that only you can do! Don't be too much of a perfectionist! Occasionally, good enough really is that.*

Elaine *Talking about it all now makes me realise how tucked away those memories are now. It was an ordeal but it's in the past, and at least the majority* *of the children's lives has been spent growing up with just me but in comfortable, calm surroundings. I could never regret marrying my ex because I've got these two wonderful children. So don't regret what you've done in life.*

Kayleigh I hope I don't sound too negative as it was a difficult role being a single parent, as you well know. As difficult as it was, when I heard the voice of this little person that I brought into this world say "I love you" it always melted my heart. Those three words could always comfort me and remind me of the blessings I had. And I'd get strength from that and it would bring things back in focus. I couldn't imagine my life without my son. I feel that I sometimes remember how difficult it was but forget how lucky I was, and am.

Annabel Being practical helps. I'm also lucky in that I'm just the kind of person who always looks forward and doesn't dwell on the past. I can't even remember half the awful things that happened. They're just not that important to me now, and I just don't bother. I'm not saying that you can choose the kind of person that you are, but what you can do is to do lots of NLP and stuff, use the positive language. No matter what terrible things might have happened, something good will come out of it. And it will be really surprising. It'll come from left field and you won't have been expecting it. You can release so much. Counselling was fantastic for me. I was told by someone, whilst sitting in her kitchen (she's the kind of person you can really trust—really clever and really nice) I was at my lowest ebb ever and she said to me:" In two years' time everything will have changed. You may not even be with someone but it won't matter because you'll be really happy. It will all be behind you. You will have learnt to cope with all of it and you will just fly". And I believed her. And it came true.

"Bad things do happen; how I respond to them defines my character and the quality of my life. I can choose to sit in perpetual sadness, immobilized by the gravity of my loss, or I can choose to rise from the pain and treasure the most precious gift I have-life itself."

—Walter Anderson

"Be happy for this moment. This moment is your life."

—Omar Khayyam

ABOUT THE AUTHOR

Vivienne Smith is a writer, trainer, presenter, transformational coach and certified NLP and Hypnosis practitioner. She also a Regional Director of the Athena Group, an international networking, training and development business community for female executives and entrepreneurs.

"Once upon a time I was perfectly happy - complacent, even. But then my world came crashing down and I was suddenly a single mum of two small children, losing sleep over how to pay the bills. My health suffered and my weight yoyo-ed as I tried to get my life in order. Luckily I'd done a lot of personal development through books and CDs and with the help of skilled practitioners. The things I learned allowed me to retain my sanity, self-esteem and sense of humour and to help my children get through the experience. I discovered how to release the traumatic experiences and emotions that were holding me back, get my weight under control and find more fun, fulfilment and balance in my life (not to mention my lovely husband!) Because I know from personal experience how challenging life can be this allows me to empathise with my clients' and readers' problems and worries and I love to help them create the life they deserve".

Her experience as a single mum prompted Vivienne to write a book about the subject. It has been the fulfilment of a long term ambition to turn what was at the time a negative and distressing experience into an opportunity to help others get through similar challenges. Now happily remarried, she lives with her husband and two sons in beautiful West Sussex, on the south coast of England.

RESOURCES:

Help and advice for single mothers

United Kingdom

Gingerbread

Gingerbread is a national charity that works for and with single parent families to improve their lives. The charity provides a freephone helpline for advice on issues affecting single parents.

- Helpline: 0808 802 0925
- Website: www.gingerbread.org.uk

Parentline Plus

Parentline Plus is a national charity providing help and support to anyone caring for children, for families living together as well as apart. It runs a freephone helpline and has a community of parents supporting each other through forums and blogs.

- Helpline: 0808 800 2222
- Website: www.parentlineplus.org.uk

Lone Parents

This support site aims to provide a virtual meeting place for single lone parent mums and dads, thereby helping to reduce the isolation and loneliness that lone single parents sometimes feel. The site provides a means for individuals to make new friends, gain advice and support through the chat rooms and forums, as well as through the Dating Site. The Site also provides practical advice and support through links to other resources—Job Centre, New Deal, CAB and a Counselling Directory, helping our members to help themselves by providing information that may otherwise be inaccessible.

Website: http://www.lone-parents.org.uk

Refuge
Refuge is a national charity that provides emergency accommodation and support for women and children experiencing domestic violence. Some of the refuges are for women of specific cultural backgrounds.
*   Website: www.refuge.org.uk

National Domestic Violence Freephone Helpline
To talk to someone in confidence for support, information or an emergency referral to temporary accommodation, contact the free 24 hour National Domestic Violence Helpline.
*   Helpline: 0808 2000 247
*   Website: www.nationaldomesticviolencehelpline.org.uk/

Al-Anon Family Groups
Al-Anon Family Groups provide support to anyone whose life is, or has been, affected by someone else's drinking, regardless of whether that person is still drinking or not. For some of their members, the wounds still run deep, even if their loved one may no longer be a part of their lives or have died. They believe alcoholism affects the whole family, not just the drinker. They are an international organisation with over 800 support groups in the UK and Republic of Ireland. Al-Anon is a fellowship of relatives and friends of alcoholics who share their experience in order to solve their common problems.
*   Helpline: 020 7403 0888
*   Website: http://www.al-anonuk.org.uk

The Down's Syndrome Association (DSA)
The only organisation in England, Wales and Northern Ireland which supports people with Down's Syndrome at every stage of life.
*   Helpline: 0333 1212 300
*   Website: http://www.downs-syndrome.org.uk

U.S.A.

The Single Parents Alliance of America provides financial assistance to single mothers. Members have access to help through grants, a pharmacy discount card and discount shopping information. Financial help is also available on an individual basis. Membership is free with proof of single parenthood.

- Website: http://www.spaoa.org/

singleparents.org is a website with advice on finances, education, parenting and relationships, including useful articles written by other single parents.

- Website: http://www.singleparents.org/

The Hotline
For victims of domestic abuse; to provide crisis intervention, safety planning, information and referrals to agencies in all 50 states, Puerto Rico and the U.S. Virgin Islands.

- Website: http://www.thehotline.org/

National Down Syndrome Society

- Website: http://www.ndss.org/

Al-Anon Family Groups
Strength and hope for friends and families of problem drinkers.

- Website: http://www.al-anon.alateen.org/

Canada

One Parent Families Association of Canada
Advice, education, social events and activities for the wellbeing of one parent families

- Website: http://www.meetup.com/oneparentfamilies/

Australia

Single with Children
A non-profit social and resource group operated by the Single Parent Family Association
- Website: http://www.singlewithchildren.com.au/SPFA-SupportGroups. shtml

National Sexual Assault, Family & Domestic Violence Counselling Line
- 24 hour service: 1800 RESPECT or 1800 737 732
- Website: http://www.dvrcv.org.au/support-services/national-services/

Al-Anon Family Groups
Strength and hope for friends and families of problem drinkers.
Website: http://www.al-anon.org/australia/

Down Syndrome Australia
- Website: http://www.downsyndrome.org.australia/

NLP and Hypnosis practitioners – contact your nearest practitioner for your FREE ONE HOUR SESSION!
Most of the practitioners listed work face-to-face as well as via telephone or via Skype

ENGLAND
Vivienne Smith
East and West Sussex
www.thelifeyoudeserve.co.uk
vivienne@thelifeyoudeserve.co.uk
UK callers: 07811 956146
International callers: + 44 (0)7811 956146

IRELAND

    Stella Vegas

    Drogheda

    www.astrologyontheweb.org

    stella_star@live.com

    +353 87 924 38 16

U.S.A

    Benny R. Ferguson Jr.

    Winston-Salem, North Carolina

    www.TheFergusonCompany.com

    benny@thefergusoncompany.com 1+336-546-7142

    Dawn Tarter

    Cuba, Illinois

    www.dawntartercoaching.com

    dtarter@rio-express.net.

    309 789 2839

CANADA

    Sabine Mohr

    Nova Scotia

    Sabine@projectnowinternational.com

    +1 902 350 2333

    Shelley Palik

    British Columbia

    www.headstartonlife.com

    shelley@headstartonlife.com

    250 804 2712

AUSTRALIA
Gary Ellbourn
Byron Bay, New South Wales
Facebook - Entheos-NLP
www.entheos-nlp.com
0468 463 390

BIBLIOGRAPHY

Bristow, Wendy, **Single and loving it.** Thorsons 2000.

Sedacca, Rosalind, **Coping with Co-Parenting Challenges After Divorce: Keep the Kids in Mind**. http://www.childcentereddivorce.com

Sedacca, Rosalind. **How Do I Tell the Kids about the Divorce? A Create-a-Storybook Guide to Preparing Your Children – with Love!** http://www.howdoitellthekids.com

Brown and Krasny Brown. **Dinosaurs Divorce: A Guide for Changing Families (Dino Life Guides for Families).** Little, Brown Books for Young Readers; Reprint edition (1988)

Pearson, Marina, **Goodbye Mr Ex** Ecademy Press Ltd 2013.

Pearson, Alison, **I Don't Know How She Does It**. Anchor 2003.

Sedacca and Sherman, **Smart Dating Advice for Women Over 40: Answers to Your Most-Asked Questions** Free e-book from: http://www.womendatingafter40.com/about.php

Covey, Stephen R, **The 7 Habits of Highly Effective Families**. Golden Books 1997

Biktashev, Moran and Yu, **The Complete Idiot's Guide to Feng Shui, 3rd Edition (Complete Idiot's Guides (Lifestyle Paperback)** Alpha Books, 3 edition, 2005

Lockwood, Georgene, **The Complete Idiot's Guide to Organizing Your Life.** ALPHA; 5 edition , 2010

Roche, Jonathan, **The No Excuses Diet: The Anti-Diet Approach to Crank up your Energy & Weight Loss!**; available on.Amazon.com

Livitnoff, Sarah, **The Relate Guide to Starting Again – how to learn from the past for a better future**, new edition.Vermilion, 2001.